Middlework:

Unlock the Underestimated and Unappreciated Secret to Success

By Matthew Hart

Contents

Introduction. 1

Be The Middle—Don't Just be In The Middle 5
Complicated, High-reward Endeavors Take a Team 6
Where do we go from here? 7

Chapter 1
The Work of the Middle 9

The Middle is a Type of Work 9
Middlework: a Simple Definition. 10
Middlework: NOT about "Ensuring Execution" 11
The Seven Behaviors of Great Middlers 13
The Six Calibrations of Great Middle Managers. 14
In the Middle of The Company 14
The Middle of the Organization: Getting Perspective 16
The Middle: From the Top 17
The Middle: From the Bottom 17
Middle Management From Their Own Point of View. 18
Organizations in the Middle. 19
Middlework and Results. 20

Chapter 2
The Seven Behaviors of
Great Middle Managers 23

1: Focus on the Greater Good. 24
2: Seek Reality 28
3: Commit to Listening. 31
4: Maintain Composure 36

5: Display Courage 44
6: Remain Flexible 45
7: Act Decisively 46
Behavior Intensity 49

Chapter 3
The Six Calibrations of Great Middlers 53

Intra-team Cohesion 54
Inter-team Cohesion 57
Top-Down Direction 59
Bottom-up Direction 59
Budget 63
Timelines and Deadlines 64
The Six Calibrations: the Really Hard Part 65

Chapter 4
The People in the Middle 67

Middle Management: Starting from the Bottom 68
Line Managers: Middlers in the Trenches 69
Senior Managers: The Toughest Gig in the World 71
Middle Management: Near the top 73
Directors 74
Vice Presidents: Kings of the Middle 75
The "P" Managers: The most important middle work
in your company 78
Organizational Structure: A Primer 83
The four dimensions: mapping the current state
to the steady state 85
Set a timeline, plateaus, and measures 86
Organizational Structure: People in the Middle 88
Determining span of control 92

Chapter 5
Get to the Middle and Make it Better 95

Set the stage 95
Eliminate entitlement. 96
Get your head out of the sand. 99
Act the part before you have the part. 100
State your intentions. 101
Do the work before you get paid for the work 101
Strive for Networking and Visibility 102
Treat the role with respect 106
Remember why you got into the business
in the first place 107
Building a Better Middle 107

Conclusion
Moving through the Middle 113

Moving through the Middle. 113
Can I do more good for the company where I am now? 114
Know the middle before you know top 114
Middlework: Breaking through the stereotypes 115

Bibliography 117

Index 119

Other Titles by Matthew Hart. 123

The Last Iteration of Dexter Maxwell 123
Oracle Enterprise Manager 10g. 124
Oracle RMAN 11g: Backup and Recovery 124

About the Author. 125

Acknowledgements

I wouldn't have been able to even notionally conceive of this book if it hadn't been for a number of great middlers I've been honored to work for and with. So here's a shout-out to John Donlin, for intervening at the right moment; Martin Ingram, for always trusting in my potential (even when it was deeply buried); and Casey Birtwell, who taught me how to truly change things.

As for the creation process itself, I owe a huge debt to Carl Knerr, for reading this and providing great advice. Some of the best parts of this book came directly from his criticism. I also need to thank Mary Silwance, for editing and fixing my broken English—all remaining mistakes are mine, not hers, left in at my insistence.

Finally, this book would never have made it without Beth Flemington from Beth Flemington Designs, who turned into a true collaborator as this book made its way from my brain and onto paper. She provided input on every chapter as a reader, made all the illustrations, designed the cover, laid out the pages, and, in other words, took this from ideas scratched to paper and actually turned it all into a book.

As always, I wrote this book while doing about ten other things that were just as important. This meant early mornings, late nights, and sacrifices around the house. Thanks to my wife and kids for understanding and supporting all of my passions.

Finally, I want to thank you for reading this book. Without readers, an author is just another monkey at a typewriter.

Middlework:

Unlock the
Underestimated and Unappreciated
Secret to Success

Introduction

I am a middle child. Not just between a couple of siblings, I am literally the center: I have two older brothers, and two younger brothers. Dead in the middle. Interestingly, when this comes up in conversation, people tip their head to one side, sympathetically, and nod a bit. As if to say, "Oh darling, you poor thing. That must have been hard."

It's got me scratching my head. I don't have a chip on my shoulder about being a middle child. Things didn't seem that different for me. But there is a generally held impression that life is tough for middle children.

> We're the middle children of history, man.
> — Tyler Durden, Fight Club

Where does that attitude come from? What does it mean to be a middle child and why do people feel it is a disadvantaged position? And more important to this book, are there lessons to be learned for other positions in the middle: middle management within companies, for instance. I believe there is a parallel and it can shed excellent light on not only what the middle is to business, but how to take advantage of its power to make strong organizations.

As I thought about this question of middle children, I stumbled across a fascinating study of middle children by Catherine Salmon, PH.D, and Katrin Schumann titled *The Secret Power of Middle Children*. Turns out, there's a media perception of a so-called "Middle Child Syndrome," characterized by "neglect, resentment, low creativity, lack of career focus, a negative outlook on life, [and] the feeling that they don't belong." (45)

And, it turns out, this sentiment in our society doesn't end at birth order. The level of pity extends to other things that are in the middle. Just take the poor middle manager: disrespected at every turn, typically sneered at by individual contributors in an organization and looked down upon by high level executives. Why would anyone want that work?

I want to claw my way up to middle management.
-- child in Monster.com commercial

The literature and articles certainly paint an even tougher picture of middle management than it does of middle children. In most cases, middle management is painted as simply irrelevant to modern knowledge industries: folks self-manage and you just need "Leaders, not managers" (David K. Williams, Forbes. com). New industries are "flat" and can no longer be "managed by looking at it" ("Saving David Brent", Economist.com).

The bottom line is that, at best, leadership tolerates middle managers and constantly looks for ways to eliminate them. What good do they do but drive up the cost of things?

But the literature and viewpoints don't tell the whole story. There is a growing body of literature and experiences pointing to the fact that the middle is more than just the punch line of the joke; the middle may, in fact, be the secret sauce of success. An interesting study by Ethan Mollick shows that having a strong, healthy middle management layer makes an appreciable difference to the bottom line. But not, by the way, in stodgy old industries. Mollick studied the video game industry. In Silicon Valley. His conclusion?

> "...I find that variation among middle managers has a particularly large impact on firm performance, much larger than that of those individuals who are assigned innovative roles.... The results also show that middle managers are necessary to facilitate firm performance in creative, innovative, and knowledge-intensive industries." (Mollick 2)

Wait a second, good middle managers have a larger impact on performance than innovators? Say it ain't so! Somebody call Jony Ive and let's get scrappy up in here!

Let's return to our poor child suffering from Middle Child Syndrome. Like the middle manager, this child has no hope, and suffers from neglect, gloom, and therefore massive amounts of therapists' bills. Right?

Wrong. Salmon and Schumann point out this simply doesn't bear out under scrutiny. Once the facts are reviewed, a different picture of middleborn children emerges. What makes a middle child's birth order so indicative of their personality and character is also the source of great power and strength—both for themselves and their relationships.

> In reality, contrary to expectations, middleborns are agents of change in business, politics, and science—more so than firstborns and lastborns. Middles are self-aware team players with remarkable diplomatic skills. Because they're both outgoing and flexible, they tend to deal well with others—in the workplace and at home. (Salmon and Schumann 47)

This is a relief for those of us of the middleborn persuasion. More important to the thesis of this book, however, is this question: what if the same power and strength of those born in the middle extended to positions in an organization?

I believe we can use the strengths of middleborns as an extended metaphor for the middles of organizations and projects. What a middleborn child is imbued with because they come from the middle, are also the traits that make for effective middle management: agents of change, self-aware team players, diplomatic, outgoing and flexible. But I'll get back to that in Chapter 1.

It's more than just about traits. It's also about the kinds of things Mollick found in his study about the power of middle management.

> "Rather than acting as cogs in the machine, dwarfed by organizational level effects, the effect of managers on firm performance was actually larger than that of organizational factors, implying that individual managerial differences play an outsized role in firm performance, even over the $4 billion in revenue generated by games in the sample." (Mollick 25)

It's time we took a fresh look at the middle. Not just because great things are happening in the middle, but rather, great things happen because of the middle. Whether it's a family, a company, or a country a healthy middle is the glue that binds successful endeavors together and sees them through to completion.

It's time we stop disrespecting the middle and start celebrating it.

"Please save any questions for later, when the grief counselor gets here."

Be The Middle—Don't Just be In The Middle

In this book, I intend to show you what it means to not only be in the middle, but to be the middle—and why that's an important distinction. Whether it's longevity or just plain old-fashioned execution that a company seeks, having strength in the middle is the secret sauce that differentiates great endeavors from the pack.

For the record: I'm not disputing that strong leadership and great leaders make a difference. Nor would I claim leadership and a strong middle can succeed in the absence of brilliant, hard-working, creative individual contributors. But, regardless of the detractors and their claims, it is the middle that will make or break a company. Why?

Complicated, High-reward Endeavors Take a Team

Okay, some things don't need people in the middle. If you want to eat, you can make yourself a sandwich. Want to write a book? Just start writing. If you want to take a drive to enjoy autumn trees, just hop in the car and go.

If you didn't feel me setting that trap, sorry. Totally meant to do it. While you may not require a middle to do any of the things above, someone else did. To get that food into the refrigerator took a team. To get the refrigerator took a team. So did the utensils. What about that book you're writing? Even if you aren't writing it on a computer (massively complicated team), someone still had to make the paper and the pencil you are using. Then there's the whole getting the thing published. And enjoying that solo trip in the car? Don't get me started.

In the end, a team is required to allow any of these things to happen. In some cases, large complex teams across multiple organizations operating out of different companies. Why do that? Why bother with the headache of such endeavors?

Because they are extremely fruitful.

Sandwiches taste good. Writing feels great. The autumn

color north of my home is gorgeous. I'm willing to part with all kinds of money to ensure I can have and do these things. Relax: I'm not going any further with the "trade money for goods and services" refresher. Just making the point that it takes a team of differently skilled people to do these things. And when there's a team, there are complications.

And when there are complications, there's a middle.

Where do we go from here?

To be successful as the middle, to embrace the power of what the middle brings to a company and to leverage it for successful endeavors, we need to define what it is, what it is not, and perhaps most importantly, how to identify a great middle in the wild. So that's chapter one.

Then, in chapter 2, it's time to dive into things a little deeper and look at the behaviors of great middle workers. Successful middlers focus on the greater good, seek reality, commit to listening, maintain composure, display courage, remain flexible, and act decisively. After looking at the characteristics that need to be nurtured, we move in Chapter 3 to focus on the activities that great middle workers focus on: the six calibrations that keep activity moving toward success.

In chapter 4, we take our characteristics and calibration activities and we put them into the context of the positions inside companies most associated with the middle: middle management. What can we learn? What can we make better?

Finally, in chapter 5, we discuss what this ultimately means to us: what does it mean to move to the middle of a company? How can I get there? What should I do to be ready? And after I get there, what's beyond the middle?

I don't just want to put the middle on display and show it's potency. I believe it's just as critical to get the right people there and keep them there.

Let's get started.

Chapter 1

The Work of the Middle

Okay. So there it is: the middle is the glue. You need it to succeed. But, what, exactly, is the middle?

First of all, every team, every company, every industry has one. Look long enough, and you will find it, whether in a company of 10, 100 or 100,000 employees. And you might be surprised: it is easier to identify in small organizations than large ones. So if these folks are all over, how do we recognize them in the wild? What are the key characteristics to take note of?

Before we can answer that, we need to first address what it is, exactly, that middlers do.

The Middle is a Type of Work

Let me say it again. First and foremost, the middle is a type of work. Regardless of where it is done or who is doing it, the middle is a set of functions that must be done for large endeavors to succeed.

Large, complicated endeavors can rarely be done alone. And as soon as you need to coordinate the efforts of multiple people, the work of the middle comes in. This is what I've come to call middlework; the set of activities, passions and commitments that must be done for endeavors to be successful.

We need to identify middlework to determine if a company has a healthy middle built for success. If we start by looking at organizational charts, we are bound to fail. In great companies who know what they are, what they need to accomplish and have respected the middle, you will find that org charts and middlework typically align.

Middlework: a Simple Definition

When I talk on the subject, my first order of business is to distinguish between the work of the middle and organizations of the middle. Sometimes middle managers do this work and sometimes they don't. Sometimes, the work of the middle is performed by individual contributors in a 'matrix management' structure—think of project managers assigned to see a project through to completion. Sometimes you will see VPs and even C-levels doing it. Okay, not often. But some people can't help themselves (and that's okay).

What is it that they are doing? Put as simply as possible, middlework is calibrating activity in the direction required to achieve the best results. The doers are going to do. That's why they are the doers. But doing needs calibration for all kinds of reasons: it's not good enough, it's not fast enough, or the industry just changed, or more is needed, less is needed, innovation happened, standards changed, rules changed, the deciders changed the decision, or they ran out of money, or are flush with new money, demand went up, demand went down, forecasts changed, weather changed, a butterfly beat its wings in Mexico City. Doers gonna do, directors gonna direct-- and calibrators gonna calibrate.

Sound simple? Even simplistic? You bet. But as I often tell

folks in my seminars, simple isn't easy. If it were, everything would be simple.

> *"Simplicity is the ultimate sophistication."*
> *-- Leonardo da Vinci*

Middlework: NOT about "Ensuring Execution"

It would be easy to add one very straightforward qualifier to my middlework definition: that not only do good middlers calibrate, they ensure execution. They are looking after the doing and ensuring it gets done.

That's not far from the truth, but it's actually not true of a good middler. It is one of the myths of middle management that has led to so many of the clichés and stereotypes. In fact, it's so widespread that I've seen it in job descriptions before, and I've heard middle managers tell me that it's their job. Yikes.

Here's why great middle managers don't see their job as ensuring work gets done: no one wants to be in the surveillance business. And no one wants to be in the surveilled business. No one respects the gang boss on a chain gang. No one wants a whip cracking across one's back.

And that is what's implied when you make the middle manager the person responsible for execution: you turn them into plantation overseers, and you turn the individual contributors into the help.

Sound extreme? Probably. I'm prone to hyperbole at time. But it's true. This one implicit (or explicit) job description that upper management puts on middle management, and that Individual Contributors (ICs) have come to expect, is perhaps the single biggest organizational disease that plagues large scale, complex endeavors.

Yeah, you can't tolerate laziness. You have to hold people accountable for their responsibilities. But if you think it takes one human to watch over another just to make sure the second one is doing what they said they would do, you have fallen victim to the villain Waste. And not just waste, but you've infantilized the IC. You've created a dependency on someone else to tell him or her how to do his or her job. It's like parents that never make their kids get themselves out of bed. How does the kid ever learn how to rouse himself?

Avoiding X management in a Y world

Whether they admit it or not, many leaders have decided to take the route of the X management style in the 'XY' theory of management, put forward by Douglas McGregor in 1960. McGregor said (and I'm paraphrasing here) there are only two kinds of management: X and Y. X is authoritarian and assumes all employees hate work and will not do it unless you make them. Y management is participatory and assumes hard work comes naturally to people if you can bring them into the process. Most leaders I talk to and consult with have the impression that they are running a Y shop, even as they expect their middle managers to perform X activities, like keeping track of complicated daily activity charts, checking to see who shows up on time, who is in their cubicle at the end of the day, etc. These activities don't encourage participation,;they engender mistrust.

So, stay away from surveillance-based ideas and stick with my definition: middlers calibrate work in the direction required to achieve the desired outcome. Once that calibration is done, any great middler knows that there's only one thing left to do: get the hell out of the way.

The Seven Behaviors of Great Middlers

We can't separate the work middlers do from the defining behaviors that make them great. These characteristics not only exist in every great middler, but in my observations, they are critical to success and therefore must be nurtured and strengthened by anyone interested in getting real results. Without these, middlers are nothing more than the clichés that exist for them.

The behaviors of a great middler are:

- Focus on the Greater Good
- Seek Reality
- Commit to Listening
- Maintain Composure
- Display Courage
- Remain Flexible
- Act Decisively

We will explore each of these characteristics in depth in Chapter 2, but keep them in mind as we look again at the calibration work of great middlers.

The Six Calibrations of Great Middle Managers

So, we know that certain traits are visible in great middlers. And we have our middlework definition: calibrating activity in the direction required to achieve the best results. But what calibrations are we talking about here? The term 'calibration' gets plenty of use in business-talk. And I'm no different. I'm using the term both in its real sense, which is "to ensure the accuracy of something," but also in the "business-world-totally-destroyed-the-meaning-but-there's-no-going-back" sense: to monitor, then make necessary changes to ensure an endeavor stays on track.

The areas that require calibration by great middlers are:

- Intra-team cohesion
- Inter-team cohesion
- Top-down direction
- Bottom-up direction
- Budget changes
- Timelines and Deadlines

We will dive into what that calibration work looks like in Chapter 3.

In the Middle of The Company

But who is doing all this middlework in global companies? And what do they look like?

We are going to be sorely tempted to look at the easiest identifiable trait of the supposed middle: where a person falls in an organizational hierarchy chart. We will want to look at the group of players that sit, by organization or work type, in between the individual contributors who do stuff and the executives who direct the stuff that needs doing. This is the oft-derided group of legend: folks who neither do the work nor decide the work to be done.

When you look at the literature, middle management is typically described as being above the line managers, or in other words, they are the managers of managers. And, you can't be at the top, or 'C level' – no one with the word "Chief" in his or her title is the middle.

However, I'm taking a little more liberal view of middle management by saying it's anyone who manages people and is also managed. Granted, I won't focus on the C-level (who needs another book about those folks?), but I want a definition that looks at the function of the middle, and not necessarily the organizational location.

The reason I am broadening the view is to ensure that we include the people who are likely doing middle work. Remember-- the middle is a type of work, while sometimes done by certain roles in company, it's important to see the calibrating actions of the middle wherever it takes place. So we will look broadly for the work in corporations.

Here's the people we are looking at: below the top folks, starting with titles like 'Area Vice President,' 'Senior Director,' or just plain old "Director." These folks are up near the top, but make no mistake: the good ones do middlework. They must be very, very good calibrators, as we will see later. Then there's the layer of an organization that is most frequently associated with the term 'middle management,' the senior manager. This person is often buried below two or more layers above, and has at least one layer below her before you find the individual contributors. The Senior Manager is, truth be told, an odd character and one that I'd argue should be used sparingly, but powerfully, in any organization. I'll get to that later in Chapter 4.

Below the senior manager is the line manager, AKA the field manager, AKA the plain old manager. Typically, this person manages the doers of an organization, filing reports, managing performance, seeing to the day-to-day needs of folks. It's easy to forget this critical function, or to assume it's a drone function, best performed by the happiest, albeit least intelligent, team member. But again we need to be very careful. Bad line management is the downfall of many, many a great company.

That should about do it, right? Not quite. There are two other roles in a company that do middlework on a daily, nay hourly basis, and to understand the work of the middle we need to spend time with them. These are the project/program managers and the product managers. I'm going to save my defense of these true warriors of the middle for Chapter 4, but here's the thesis in a nutshell: managing a project is nearly the most critical, in-the-middle role there is. I say "nearly" only because the product manager is the. Most. Critical. Member of just about any team. Hard to believe how often these two roles get taken for granted even as the wheels come off and the money stops flowing in.

The Middle of the Organization: Getting Perspective

Middlework does often happen in the middle of an organization, and so it's important that we check in with these folks and talk about what they look like, and what they should look like. One way to do this is to view it from the view from the top and then the bottom. Finally, how does the middle view itself?

The Middle: From the Top

When top executives look down at middle management, they have numerous reactions: some rational, some emotional, some positive, but many negative. Typically, middle management is seen , at best, as a necessary evil. This is the point of view taken when middlers are seen in terms of gang bosses; in place merely because the great and seeing Eye of Sauron (er, the CEO) cannot personally crack the whip across the backs of everyone on a large organization. Not to mention all the performance reviews once a year! So, she hires whip crackers.

In more positive terms, middle management is seen as a megaphone when it's time to change corporate direction, challenge the troops to achieve more, or get out the word about the most recent Big Thing that sparkled brightly enough for the CEO and her VPs to take notice. In this sense, middle management is seen as the voice of leadership, whispering into everyone's ear, and then reporting back.

In great companies, middle management is seen as both interface and advisory board. Things travel back and forth, and the degree to which there is fidelity (in both directions) is the degree to which success is maintained. As advisory board, great leadership listens to what middle managers are saying about the teams they lead and what innovations and ideas are bubbling up from the doers.

The Middle: From the Bottom

When individual contributors (IC's) look up, the perspective is as varied as the IC's themselves, and their industries. A lot depends on how those doers expect to be treated, how much freedom they have known (if any), and how good the middle management itself is.

The stereotypical response is cynical astonishment: how can that actually be a real job? What does she do all day? Why is she always telling me what to do? So many meetings. So many reports, forms, processes, surveys, emails.

More positively, doers simply tolerate middle management as the person who has to talk to upper management, give people their performance reviews, deals with that creep two cubicles over, and generally put up with the BS that inevitably comes with global companies. Better him than me, in other words.

In great companies, doers see middlers in much the same way as the top brass does: the interface and advisory board. The IC's need information to flow both vertically and horizontally across a large organization, and they also need to focus on the doing. The middle management is how competing priorities get cleared up, how protection occurs so that focus can be maintained, and how ideas can bubble up and be spread across the organization.

Middle Management From Their Own Point of View

There is also, of course, how middle managers see themselves. There is the view best described in television (The Office): the manager is there to spread good cheer, even artificially, keep everyone happy, manage reports upward and deliver news downward. The job is to watch and report.

Middle management may see their job as more engaged than that, and really pride themselves on staying hooked into daily progress with all sorts of spreadsheets and work aggregation systems. They keep an eye on performance, and push hard for results. This is the micro-management dysfunction.

Great middlers see themselves not only as an interface, but a discerning one: not all information travels up, and not all information travels down. At least, not without calibration and possible translation.

Some may point at this statement and say "Aha! Caught you, Matt! You just said great middle managers distort the information coming from ICs and from Executives! And you said it like it's a good thing! Just the reason we must flatten our organizations!"

The fear of distortion is real, and cannot always be avoided. But, members of a team, buried in their focused attention to tasks, may not hold the whole entirety of the result in their minds. Sometimes, the middle manager must find a way to translate the information so it can be processed and understood. It's not spin, its getting things done.

Organizations in the Middle

There are people in the middle of organizations and there is the middlework that has to get done in every sophisticated endeavor. Sometimes, there are also companies in the middle.

Actually, it's not sometimes. There are thousands of companies in the middle. Seriously, the de facto way to make money on the Internet for many companies is to be the middle. Craigslist. Ebay. Google.

Yes, Google. You heard me. Google isn't an end in itself. You don't go to google.com to do anything. You go there to find something else. Google's entire mission is to get you off of its search engine as quickly as possible—connected to whatever it is you are trying to find.

Even Google's more recent endeavors remain focused on connecting. One of the most successful companies of the new millennium, and it's just one really, really big middleman.

There are hundreds of great examples. One that I love talking about is Arise Virtual Solutions. Arise doesn't make anything. You don't hire Arise to do any one thing. In fact, Arise doesn't really have a lot of people that do anything for you. Instead, Arise Virtual Solutions connects two critical groups: people who need things to get done and people who are available and enthusiastic about getting those things done. Middlework is the glue, keeping great endeavors on track.

The intent of this book is not to focus on middlework companies—that's an entirely different discussion. But it's worth taking a few moments as you read this to see not only what middlework looks like, but also the huge opportunities that open up when you are aware of it.

Middlework and Results

So, there you have it: middlework is the calibrating activities required to achieve the desired outcome. This can be done by certain people in an organization or it can be done by anyone. Typically, there is a middle of an organization that is tasked with middlework. Sometimes, this work is done by companies that have decided being in the middle is not only important, but extremely profitable.

To get to a better understanding of what great middlework looks like, who should do it, and how to get better, let's get to know the behaviors of great middle managers a little better.

Chapter 2

The Seven Behaviors of Great Middle Managers

How can you recognize a great middle manager? What does he look like? Do they all have something in common? Over the past decade of observing global companies, I can answer that question with an unequivocal yes. In fact, there are seven behaviors that, when developed together, ensure a middle manager will succeed in her calibrating activities.

Not every person is the same, and this is one of the great truths about humans. We don't want every person to act exactly the same. Diversity in personality, in beliefs, in talents: these are the things that make endeavors strong. So do not think that I am advocating that all middle managers start acting the same. Nor would I assume that these seven characteristics are all that is required. But my observations have led me to consider these seven behaviors are "table stakes" for great middle management.

One more note before we dive in: these traits are, first and foremost, guiding behaviors that great middle managers display. They are behaviors that come from practice and principles that have been internalized by the managers over the course of their careers. These behaviors can and must be learned, practiced, and made stronger, like muscles. These are things that you get better at every time you use them.

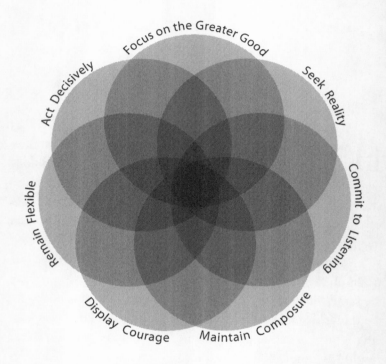

The Seven Behaviors of Great Middle Managers

1: Focus on the Greater Good

What is the greater good? This subject is a rabbit hole, to be sure, and it's hard to get to the bottom of it quickly. But it is worth spending some time on. Greater Good, with capital letters, can refer to your personal set of values. What is important to me? What matters the most?

By definition, this has to be something outside of your own self interest or I wouldn't call it the Greater Good. If what is most important to you in terms of the energy you expend is your own aggrandizement, well, that's okay at some level. But you probably won't make a very good middle manager. However, if you can attach your own vested interests and personal improvement to a larger purpose, then we are getting somewhere.

We all want to improve our station in life, whether it is through money, education, experiences or public recognition. I am not advocating a selfless lifestyle. In fact, the first trait of a great middle manager is not pure selflessness. Throwing yourself into an endeavor with no thought of your personal outcomes, your personal principles or your own life balance would be reckless and damaging. I've done that before, and I would not recommend it. Along the way, your integrity gets damaged, your family and friends get lost, and you end up burned out with no fuel left in the tank.

Instead, we need to know what it is outside ourselves that is important. First, what is important to you as a human? What matters most? This could be your family, your religion, your country. It could be a set of objectives you have for yourself or for the world in which you live. You need to define it. If you walk into any large-scale, complex endeavor without knowing what you stand for and what matters in the world outside yourself, you will be swallowed up by the endeavor itself.

Perhaps getting swallowed by the endeavor is on purpose; what you are dedicating yourself to is, in fact, the Greater Good. Fantastic. Congratulations, and I know what that feels like too.

It is powerful. But in many cases, the endeavor you are engaging in is a company or project you find exciting and you believe in, but is still separate from what matters most to you personally. So walk into it with open eyes, keeping your behavior aligned to your principles. Know your own greater good before you know that of your company.

Trading layoffs for work: the Greater Good in action

An excellent middle manager, Steve, ran a crack team of servicing engineers in a big telecommunications company. These folks were the absolute cream of the diagnostic crop: they had been slowly coming together over more than a decade of servicing this company's core suite of products, and they knew not only how they worked, but how they worked in relationship to each other and in the broader ecosystem of technology around them. If there was a problem with a major customer, this was the team you called to get the issue worked out, calm the customer down, and get everything back on track. They were outside of the process of managing standard service tickets. They were only called into action when standard processes broke down.

This was 2008 when the global economy was coming off the rails. Steve's company was no different; the word finally came from leadership: time to make cuts. The layoffs would be handled as a straight 10% cut across all teams and divisions in the Services business.

This was a tough pill for Steve to swallow. His SWAT team was at the top of the food chain; cutting 10% of the A team wouldn't serve the company well. But when he turned to the general customer service organization, the manager there, Joe, was at pains to describe how the 10% cut was going to impact his ability to manage the sheer volume of service tickets flowing in.

Steve wrestled with the issue before coming up with a tough but important trade off. He approached Joe and told him that his SWAT team would take standard service tickets based on a certain level of complexity, thereby decreasing the pressure on Joe's overall line of business. In return, he asked Joe to take the headcount cuts Steve need to make and remove them from the less-skilled end of the business.

Joe immediately saw the value in this. He knew that the Services organization relied on these 'top guns' every week to unstick the toughest issues. He agreed with Steve, and they took their plan to the Vice President. She agreed to transfer the reduction costs, Steve and Joe changed their process, and the business spun on.

Know the Greater Good in the context of your endeavor

We've discussed how to identify your Greater Good and how that relates to your company, your project and your team. But it needs to get framed in terms of the particular endeavor at hand. What does the Greater Good look like in relation to what you need to get done?

This could be as simple as achieving the goal in front of team, but it's probably not that simple. As the degree of middle increases or the amount of authority and accountability the middler is given goes up, the Greater Good gets more sophisticated than just accomplishing the work of a team. The endeavor needs to be balanced against what else is going on in the company. Are there market pressures that make on-time delivery of this product necessary? Are there dependencies in other parts of the company that need you to deliver with quality? Does the service your division provides need to shore up an unexpected bug that just occurred in the product you support? Think of Steve and his tough layoff situation. These are contextual elements of the Greater Good that the middle manager must know.

Internalizing the Greater Good

Once you understand the greater good, you have to go a step further. Once you know the context, a great middle manager must next internalize that Greater Good.

I know, I know. I just told you not to overcommit, right? That's still true, but a great middle manager still needs to take what the Greater Good is and own it. Make it the focus of the activities and work you do.

> *There is a difference between knowing the path, and walking the path.*
>
> -- *Morpheus, The Matrix (1999)*

2: Seek Reality

This sounds easier than it is. One of the biggest impediments to organizational success is often self-deception and hubris. Folks involved in an endeavor can become convinced, based on past success, that their current endeavor is on the road to success. They then look for all the evidence required to support that view. At the same time, they ignore evidence piling up that things aren't going as planned.

Leaders and doers make this mistake in equal parts. And it

Categories of fact-gathering:

- *Task list and task dependencies*
- *Budget*
- *Defects and exceptions*
- *Vendor and 3rd party dependencies*
- *Interpersonal dynamics*
- *Timeline (holidays, vacations?)*
- *Morale and team buy-in*

---

shows up in many ways, from believing a dysfunctional team is capable of moving forward, to assuming the budget is enough to complete the task, to watching timelines slip dangerously by without making adjustments.

It is everyone's job to stay out of the self-delusion trap, but there is no place where it's more important than at the middle. Middlework requires, above all else, that reality remain firmly front-of-mind.

Job one: Be a fact-gatherer

The first step to ensuring you stay grounded in reality is simple: make it a habit to gather and synthesize facts. Gathering means more than asking for reports; it means watching and listening carefully to team members, leaders, and peers (we will spend more time on Listening next). What are you listening for? What, exactly, are the facts?

Unfortunately, this is where we would be getting into the specifics of different endeavors. Facts that need to be gathered have to do with straightforward and well-polished subjects, such as task progress reports and budget burn-down lists. But we also need to gather facts on team dynamics and morale.

Job two: Be a fact synthesizer

Gathering facts is not enough by itself. Data does not create wisdom simply by the act of being collected. As facts come in, they need to be synthesized, filtered and compared in relationship to each other.

This is really the core of what great middlers do, in the end. They must analyze facts and decide if an action must be taken. We talk more about this in the next chapter, The Six Calibrations of Great Middle Managers. For now, know that synthesis is critical to avoid being taken by surprise and is the difference between adding value to an endeavor or simply being the cleric that documents and reports data.

Job three: Be fact-driven

Gather, synthesize, act. That is all I am suggesting. Not earth-shattering advice. But it bears repeating: once you have gathered and done the synthesis, you need to ensure that it is the facts that drive your actions and decisions. Humans are emotional creatures, and that emotion can be a fantastic source of motivation, drive, and accomplishment. It can also be deceptive, destructive, and create impediments. Great middle managers stay devoted to the facts in making decisions.

In one sense, a great middle manager is not that different from a very skilled diagnostician. When someone needs to diagnose an illness, a software defect, or a hardware malfunction, that person cannot be driven by what he hopes is true or what used to be true. He absolutely must adhere to the facts that are presented, must dig for more facts, must synthesize and eliminate facts that do not apply to the symptoms at hand, then act to rectify the issue based on those facts.

When you habitually use facts to make decisions, you not only make better decisions, but you engender credibility both from above and below. But sometimes this will run directly against the current of the endeavor—we'll talk about the courage requirement in just a bit.

3: Commit to Listening

Sometimes I become convinced that being a good listener is perhaps the toughest behavior to learn. Some folks I've interviewed and observed in global industry are natural listeners; others are natural talkers; others can be both. But really listening, and not just waiting for your turn to talk, is the most powerful business skill that goes unappreciated on a day-to-day basis.

There are good books on the subject, sort of. I would recommend to anyone the superb book *Crucial Conversations* by Kerry Patterson et. al. At its core, *Conversations* tries to teach people to listen carefully to others.

Seeking reality is critical to success, and that means gathering information. Facts come in all shapes and sizes, and not all of them come from or are about the other humans that make up an endeavor. But to gather all the facts that require synthesis for keeping an endeavor on track, a middle manager must interact with others involved. And she must, above all else, listen.

Being a great listener means having a high "emotional IQ." Emotional IQ means being aware of the feelings and emotions you bring to any situation. Once you know how an interaction is affecting your own emotional state, you are better equipped to listen for clues about the emotional state of others.

Great listening is about hearing three different things:

- What the person is telling you (the intended message)
- The person's emotional state in relaying the message
- What the person is not telling you (the open space)

The intended message

First and foremost, your job is to ensure you capture and understand what the intended message is. This is both obvious and harder than it seems. It could be that you are not dealing with the most effective communicator; it could be that you are dealing with someone in a compromised emotional state. Whatever the case, make sure you get the message before you move on. To get the message, you need to understand the person's emotional state and then listen for what's not being said.

Getting the Message:
Mechanisms for ensuring you have it

- *Write it down*
- *Speak the message back to the person*
- *Confirm what you heard with a 3rd party*

Understanding the emotional state

Ensure that when someone is communicating information to you, that you are keeping yourself aware of the person's emotional state. This is critical to understanding the message, as well as what it means. When discussing emotional states, I focus on three areas of emotional range:

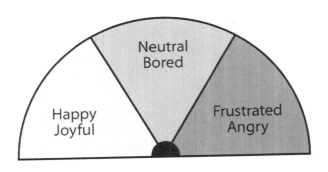

- Happy, joyful, excited
- Neutral, bored, distracted
- Frustrated, angry, agitated

Getting a feel for which of these ranges a person is in can be tricky and it may not reveal itself in a single interaction. But this needs to be ascertained to the best of your ability in order for effective calibrations to take place.

Listening for what's not being said

Last, but not least, listening is about more than getting the intended message and divining the emotional state. It's also about listening for omissions. Think about a painting, a great photograph or a movie. There's the subject of the painting itself- a mountain, a pile of fruit, a chair. But what makes great art is also the "negative space" in the picture. This is just as important to the composition as the subject itself. Think about the following picture:

"Negative Space:" A Vase or Two Faces?

This is an excellent visual example of our principle. Just as you need to look at this picture in two different ways to see the vase, then the two faces, you must also listen to people in two ways to hear what they are telling you and what is omitted. Conversations have negative space as surely as a picture does. And a great listener pays attention to what is not being said as well as what is being said.

This is important for two reasons. First, there is the unintentional omission. This is the situation where the information you need to act may not be readily apparent to the person delivering the message. For instance, take the situation from my friend Asim. At the time, he was running a small development team as a scrum master (Think of it as a highly specialized software project manager. It has nothing to do with rugby.). He was having a conversation with one of the developers, who was struggling to get a certain function developed. He kept telling Asim all of the things he was doing to get caught up, including getting the environment setup to do the development.

That caught Asim's attention. He knew, because he's a great reality-seeker, that the environmental setup was an action that was committed to his team from another organization. His developer didn't realize he was behind because someone else was stuck. Asim turned to his peers to get a sense of why the environments were not being configured correctly. It turns out, there was a much larger, more important project that had taken precedence, and it was moving so fast it had not been communicated. Asim then used his calibrating skills to make a trade off to free up his developer by getting another resource to build the development environment.

If Asim had only been listening for what his developer was reporting, he would not have been able to remove the obstacles in his way.

Getting the Message:
Mechanisms for Divining Emotional States

How do we gauge these responses? There are multiple books on this subject, but here are the cliff notes:
- *Be aware of your own emotional state*
- *Listen for emotion keywords*
- *Mind the context clues (where is the message? What are the circumstances?)*
- *Don't be afraid to address how you believe someone feels*

The second reason to listen to the open space in a conversation is because there's sometimes a tactical omission taking place. In the same way that a magician distracts her audience by keeping your eyes on her hands, sometimes the message being delivered is purposefully distracting you from something.

Trust first and assume positive intent. Not everyone is trying to hide things from his manager or purposefully deceive. But it is human nature to not want to deliver bad news. Sometimes a person is legitimately trying to get a project back on track himself and hesitates to bring up what's gone awry. Whatever the reason, great listeners must look past the message and see if there is a message NOT being delivered.

4: Maintain Composure

Things can go smoothly without any effort. Or anyway, I've heard that happens. My experience, however, is that things fall apart. Teams fight. Leaders change direction. Money runs out. Growth happens too fast, or too slow. Any of these pressures can lead to emergencies, crises, and put people on edge.

Great middle managers keep their cool at all times. Take that emotional spectrum from earlier in the chapter and look at it again. The middle manager needs to keep things around here:

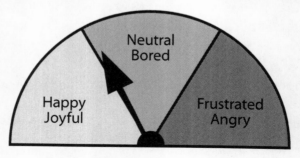

Maintaining composure does not mean being positive all the time. Eternal optimists force everyone around them to take on the role of realists and that's exhausting. On the same note, being in Neutral all the time doesn't provide any emotional feedback to the team. Let's not even get started on the managers who spend most of their time in Frustrated or Angry states-- these managers suck the air out of a team and leave behind only job-seekers and emotionally turned-off colleagues.

Granted, you cannot stay in a single emotional state all the time. Even great middlers are people, too, and deserve the right to get excited and feel joy, and the room to be frustrated or lethargic. But the rule of thumb is to always come back to the center between Joyful and Neutral. This is particularly true when others' emotional states are flaring into the red. Keeping cool is critical middlework behavior. So how to do this?

The best way to maintain composure is through the tactical use of diplomacy.

Diplomacy as fire retardant

First and foremost, diplomatic behaviors deployed before a crisis will act as a retardant for fires. Sure, crises will still flare up, but they won't overwhelm your shop. Great middle managers set the stage for cool heads by creating diplomatic relationships with key people up, across, and down the organization.

Diplomacy is a two-way street. It implies give and take; it implies a relationship. So don't mistake diplomacy for sycophancy (being a "yes man," or a "suck-up"), which is a one-way street. Diplomacy is a hard-fought and hard-won setting for ensuring peaceful coexistence and progress. Don't be a suck up. Seriously. And if you are working in an organization, or for a person, who rewards people for unilateral decision-making, you should move on.

Invest in relationships early and often

Use your listening skills to get an understanding of the needs and wants of team members, leaders, and doers that you interact with. Taking time to listen is an investment itself, but then do the next thing. Synthesize what you hear and turn it into a set of actions that gets results for that person.

When I took over a troubled development team a few years ago, the diplomatic situation was a nightmare. After years of failing to deliver, the team was on the verge of being completely shut down. My job was to assess if that was the right thing to do. But first, I had to repair some relationships.

I took a look at the portfolio of in-flight projects. Then I spoke with the folks who needed this team to perform. I asked the VP, if everything else failed, what was the one thing absolutely needed from this team?

"I need the new CRM implemented," he said. "It's been going for two years already, and we have a ton of cost savings we've already taken out of the business based on the CRM functions we were promised. If I don't get that in six months, we are in big trouble."

Of course, this project was the one in the most trouble. But I went back to the VP and I told him, "I will ensure you get CRM done in six months. That will take precedence over everything else." The VP was obviously very pleased with my answer. But then I kept going.

"To do that, I'm going to need your support," I said. "Things are going to get worse before they get better." I laid out a plan for him, showing the measurements his team could use to track our progress with the CRM integration so he would always know we were on track. Then I gave him the final ask. "I need to run steady for those six months. I can't be battling reorganizations and shrinkage until we get that done."

Ask for something in return

After you have invested, make sure you ask for something in return. It can be little, such as a decision that allows a project to move forward. It can be bigger, such as time invested in reviewing a full project budget for red flags. Make sure the ask isn't too large, at first. But make sure you ask.

The Vice President that needed his CRM agreed to support my stressed team. So we got to work and I took a number of projects and put them on the back burner.

Sure enough, the moment came. Four months into the CRM integration, and the business lead came looking for massive headcount reductions. Every division needed to put a plan together. So I gave the VP a call and we discussed what we could do together. Finally, when it was my turn to present a plan, it was not aggressive enough for the advisory committee. But the VP spoke up.

"Matt's team needs to get this CRM out the door, and he has a long-term plan for getting to a sustainable size," he said. "We need to give him more time to turn around the critical projects before we cut budget."

That was all it took. We delivered the CRM on time, and then we went on to transform every element of the team for better efficiency and execution.

People naturally desire to impact the outcome of important

endeavors, and sharing the responsibility for an outcome is one way to ensuring a crisis can be navigated as a team. Letting people into the outcome reinforces the relationship and creates the diplomatic trust required to overcome the pending crisis.

Diplomacy as firefighter

And there is always a pending crisis. It is coming. It could be small, or it could be large, but tomorrow, or the next day, or next week, you will need to flex your diplomatic muscles when emotions run hot and things need to happen quickly, or profoundly.

Leverage your investment in relationships, but also know that not everyone will react with cool heads to the crisis. In the end, there is a recipe that helps keep things cool and a crisis heading for resolution.

The cheat-sheet for diplomacy under fire

- *Assume positive intent across all players*
- *Remember your listening skills and start with listening, not talking*
- *Ask for facts from as many sources as possible*
- *Keep your eye on where authority lies (both assigned and earned authority)*
- *Formulate and articulate an opinion on the situation*
- *Always provide solutions with multiple options*

Assume Positive Intent

When a crisis is in full-blown hot-mess mode, the worst thing to do when walking into the situation is start looking for blame and fault. This almost immediately ensures people will start looking to remove themselves from the situation and your access to the facts will be damaged. Start by ensuring that your own view is not being tainted by past wrongs or what the situation looks likes—in other words, being aware of the emotions and feelings you are bringing to the situation. Sure, someone may be deliberately trying to undermine the situation. But the likelihood is low; and even if its true, you still have to carry forward in a collaborative way if you intend to get anything done.

Start with listening, not talking

Worst move ever in most crisis situations: step in and start talking like a boss. People will shutdown; if not because you are purposefully stampeding over them, then because they are relieved someone else is here to 'take over' and they can get away. Wrong. Start by asking questions, listening to the parties, and practicing the third trait. Commit to listen.

Get facts from as many different sources as possible

> *Nobody is lying, but the stories don't line up.*
> *-- Ani DiFranco*

The act of fact-gathering serves two purposes in a crisis: first, it gets people talking so you can assess the situation; second, it allows you to triangulate toward a solution. Getting the facts from a single source can be damaging and should be avoided-- not because someone is lying, but because they only have one perspective on the situation. Gather from multiple people-- it gets to the truth, and it shows diplomatic intent.

Keep your eye on where Authority Lies

There are two kinds of authority worth mentioning here because in a crisis situation you need to be extremely aware of both. First, there is assigned authority. This is the kind that comes from one's position, mostly. A Vice President has more assigned authority than a Director that reports to her. The 'business stakeholder' has assigned authority over a project outcome.

The second kind is earned authority. Put simply, earned authority is street cred. It is the authority a person gets based on their credibility in the company, between people or in the larger world.

Sometimes, assigned and earned authority are with the same person. But you can't count on it and you have to know the difference, particularly in crisis situations. Assigned authorities might be looking to get the crisis averted, but the doers are most likely looking to the Earned Authorities for direction on what to do.

It is the job of great middlers to know who is who and to navigate the dicey waters between them. When the VP jumps on the war room conference bridge demanding action, do you know where to find the Database Administrator that actually needs to determine the right action to take?

Formulate and state your opinion

Gather your data, know the players and then the moment always comes when a great middle manager knows: it's time to take a point of view. And make no mistake: even if you have nothing but cold hard evidence to support your point of view, it is still one of many points of view. And it may not be the prevalent one. But you need to formulate your point of view and then you need to make it clear.

This is your platform as a middler. If you are too afraid to take a point of view that determines and drives a plan of action then you should remove yourself from the crisis situation because you're not helping. Even if you are wrong, having a clearly articulated opinion on the situation helps others clarify their own perspectives and leads to better data sharing and better action plans.

Provide solutions, preferably with more than one option

Once you have articulated your opinion, be sure to follow up with a proposal and what you think should happen next. Big ugly problems rarely get solved by a single, monolithic solution. Instead, the solution you offer is how to move past the most pressing obstacle. Perhaps it's a mechanism to get more information so the underlying problem becomes better understood. Whatever it is, come to the table with a solution-- and even better, come with options.

Options provide a mechanism that shows you are operating outside a single line of thought. This is actually the case-- the mental act of forcing yourself to ask "what else could we do here?" gets you freed from chasing the wrong path too far.

Come with options. Options are also one the best cool-under-fire moments. Particularly where there is tough action to take (someone has to work through the weekend, so who's it going to be?), alternatives show a diplomatic readiness to discuss all other courses of action openly and fairly.

5: Display Courage

Fear is the mind-killer.

-- Frank Herbert, Dune

Formulating and stating an opinion, even when you provide multiple options, can be more dangerous than it sounds. But too little is made in the literature of management around the importance of courage. So much of bad global company culture comes from cowardice. But that cowardice springs from somewhere. It comes from the very real experience of getting burned by firmly stating an opinion that may fly in the face of common-held feelings. The very real experience of being intimidated into a different opinion. The experience of seeing facts pushed aside. Despite evidence, sometimes people are told to 'get on board.'

But, you can't put your horns down and just bull ahead. Courage without diplomacy is merely intimidation, and that's not how great middlers get things done. Courage, combined with diplomacy, creates space for facts to be evaluated and decisions to be made.

A middle manager must have reserves of bravery to rely on. There's plenty of places that such bravery can come from: laying the foundation with strong relationships (diplomacy), listening and ensuring you have all the facts, and keeping your eye on authority. In other words, the traits that make a great middle manager are also the traits that build reserves of courage.

Courage without diplomacy is no good, but the opposite is also true: diplomacy without courage is sycophancy, and that leads to self-deception. Self-deception is the killer of progress.

6: Remain Flexible

It takes courage to make decisions; it takes greater courage to admit mistakes, change your mind publicly and move in a different direction. This is what I refer to as the behavior of flexibility. Don't mistake it for being a pushover; we've discussed above why that won't be the case for great middle managers. But it is critical to not only be flexible, but to be visibly so.

Flexibility starts with humility

It would be hard to overstate the importance of humility in remaining flexible and open to different points of view; different ways of doing business, different ways of accomplishing tasks, and different ways of ensuring the endeavor finds success. Humility is the characteristic of allowing that you are not the only person with great ideas, you are not the best that you don't know everything. When put that way, it sounds like a no-brainer, right? But often we associate humility with weakness or a lack of judgment. But that is not the case for great middlers. There is strength that comes from internalizing the Greater Good and from knowing and synthesizing the facts. There is courage to judge the situation and make decisions to ensure positive outcomes.

The humble middler does not rush to judgment too soon,

and even after making a decision, remains open to the possibility that a change may have to be made. More facts will emerge that might require calibration. This is the ongoing act of flexibility: one part humility, one part diplomacy, two parts courage.

Flexibility is both an enabler of the six other traits we are discussing, but also an outcome of them. There is a positive feedback loop that gets created when you begin to nurture these traits together and combine them into a set of ongoing behaviors you exhibit in the workplace.

7: Act Decisively

The capability to act decisively is more nuanced than it typically sounds, but the hardest part for most middle managers is that decisiveness requires her to judge the situation. And judgment sounds like a BIG DEAL. It sounds like something that folks in black robes and with stern looks do. But this is not the case. Using sound judgment is often no more than providing an intelligent opinion, a firmly stating a point of view. But it does require having a point of view.

Knowing the Greater Good, staying grounded in reality, listening carefully and openly, and investing in diplomacy: these are the foundations of a great middle manager. Sooner or later, however, all of this leads up to that manager doing something which can be uncomfortable, but entirely necessary: passing judgment.

Judging someone, or something, before you have all the facts is never good. Sometimes we rely on personal biases. Sometimes we rely on how that person has acted in the past even if the situation is entirely different. But there are times, particularly in the middle, when judgment must be rendered.

You've gathered the facts first, of course, but now it's time for action. Decisions precipitate execution.

We act decisively all the time. Where will I eat dinner tonight? Where will I shop for groceries? What book should I read next? Sometimes, we make these decisions without consciously practicing great middle behaviors. But sometimes they are required. A good friend, Carl, once described the process he went through with his spouse to make a decision on where they sent their kids to school. It took diplomacy, courage, reality, and composure, not to mention flexibility and, in the end, decisiveness. In the professional world, this could be as straightforward as making a decision on how to resolve an intra-team dispute. Let me give you an example.

Two different development managers had been angling to be the lead on the same high-profile project. This was a project that potentially equated to tens of millions of dollars to our company and it was a multi-year project that the manager could stay focused on without other distractions. It only needed one lead even though the preceding project had involved both of these men.

I had the facts. I knew the diplomatic fall-out from choosing one or the other and what the impact would be to my team's dynamics. In the end, it was a judgment call.

But I didn't make it. I wasn't sure which direction to go. I kept divvying up components of the larger project and handing them to both of the managers. It was a disaster.

Both managers resented the parts that went to the other, so I was constantly trying to calibrate intra-team issues. And in the end, because I wouldn't put someone in charge, it meant I was in charge-- a situation I honestly didn't have time for.

This is where flexibility comes in. I realized the mistake,

albeit late, and changed the dynamic. I put one in charge and moved the other to a set of smaller projects. The immediate impact was painful, but everyone recovered and the project started to really sail along. Just as important, my two team members became much more tolerable around each other.

Some decisions can be far tougher when you are in the middle. It can deeply impact someone's life.

I've hinted at the tough work I did in 2008 and 2009 when the US economy hit a brick wall. I took over a struggling development organization at the same time that the company had to shed thousands of jobs to stay solvent. I had to streamline the organization, which meant I was in charge of cutting my budget in half. When you are a development shop the only way to turn the dial on your budget is to cut jobs.

The process of judging which people would remain at the company and which ones would get the exit package was the toughest thing I've done in my career. This is not like working through a dispute; this is putting someone's family in a tough situation.

But the work had to be done. If I didn't do it, someone else would, and perhaps someone with less of an eye for what the team needed in order to succeed. So I went through an exhaustive due diligence process. I flew all over the globe to different offices where the team worked. In the end, we didn't just slice a percentage off the team. Instead, we transformed the team, negotiated a smaller workload with our stakeholders, streamlined processes, and eliminated roles that could be performed elsewhere in the business. Then, I looked at who was needed to make the new team succeed.

And then, a thousand hours into the process, we made the list and started informing people of the tough news.

Great Managers are Great because they Decide

Great middle managers don't rush to judgment but they do not shy away from it either. Mediocre or bad managers are easy to recognize in the ecosystem, because they are nothing more than a pass-through for information. When a decision is required, they ask someone else. When there is judgment necessary, they find someone else to do it. They are a doorway, and nothing else.

Nurturing good judgment is not a simple task; it is something that you could write an entire book about. But the behaviors I am describing in this chapter lay the foundation for great judgment: know what the Greater Good is. Stay fact-based and fact-driven. Listen carefully and openly. Nurture diplomatic, two-way relationships.

In the end, however, the test of great judgment comes in two ways. First, that you actually make the judgment. And second, that you are willing to be wrong, admit it, and make a change. Both of these require the final two traits of great middle managers: courage and flexibility.

Behavior Intensity

One of the interesting observations I've made in my studies of great middle managers is what I call "Behavior Intensity." What I mean by that is while all seven behaviors of great middle managers must be present at all times, as the span of responsibility increases or decreases, you see different intensities of these behaviors.

Take, for instance, the Senior Director of a major software development division at a technology firm. She needs to spend more time managing conflicting priorities (knowing the greater good) than she does ensuring she remains as flexible as possible.

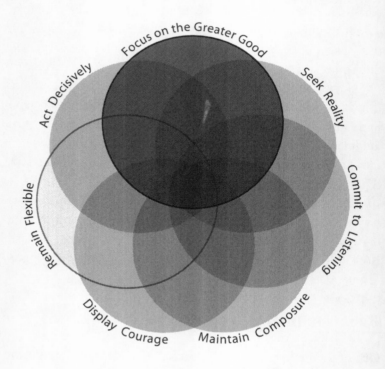

A Senior Director prioritizes her Focus on the Greater Good

The opposite case: the brand new line manager, just promoted from his role as an individual contributor, needs to focus on listening and diplomacy more than flexing her courage and judgment muscles.

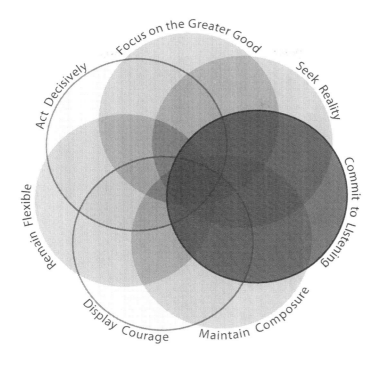

A new line manager emphasizes his Commitment to Listening

As you take on a new role, it is critical you take a look at the seven traits and ensure you know which behaviors to focus on. Once you have done that, and you've turned these characteristics into habits, it's time to focus on the work you will be doing: the calibrations of great middlers.

Chapter 3

The Six Calibrations of Great Middlers

Over the course of my two decades in global companies, as well as in my research and discussions with others, I've come to see six critical areas great middle managers must keep accurately calibrated. There are certainly more than six activities that good middlers deploy, but the basic categories of good calibration are:

- Intra-team Cohesion
- Inter-team Cohesion
- Top-down Direction
- Bottom-up Direction
- Budget Changes
- Timelines and Deadlines

Keeping your eyes on these six areas is like having your eye on the dashboard of a car, or in the cockpit of a plane. These are the core dials you will need to be constantly adjusting to keep endeavors on track.

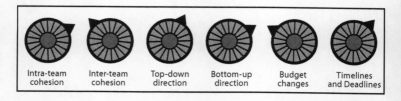

| Intra-team cohesion | Inter-team cohesion | Top-down direction | Bottom-up direction | Budget changes | Timelines and Deadlines |

The Six Calibration Dashboard

What's important about the control panel metaphor is that there's no 'right place' for these settings. What you need to calibrate in each of these areas will depend heavily on the endeavor you are steering to completion.

Intra-team Cohesion

Things fall apart. And teams do too. In fact, keeping a functioning team on the same page, working toward the same goal, takes leadership and constant vigilance.

The Finger-wag trap

Perhaps the biggest impediment to good teamwork is the battle of egos. Let me share a story from Lisa, who at the time was VP of Software Development, accountable for the development and release of new internal functionality. This wasn't product, so to speak, but rather the unique systems that are required to support the company's core business.

When Lisa took over Development she had two "A" players on her staff, Jessica and Anil. Both were the kinds of people that anyone wants on a team: intelligent, passionate, and hard working. There was only one problem.

Jessica and Anil hated each other.

No use diving into all the history on exactly how Jessica and Anil came to such a place; they had been working together for over a year when Lisa took over the division. At first, Lisa couldn't even see the animosity as personal; it had been so built into how Jessica and Anil's teams interacted with each other that all Lisa could see was operational overlap, broken process, and blame as far as the eye could see.

After trying to work through the issues for a few months, it finally became clear to Lisa that her two best players were not interested in allowing the other to succeed. Any chance they found, they would let the other team fail in an effort to get the other out of the business.

Lisa pulled them individually into a room and confronted the animosity head-on, explaining that she was clearing the past, it was a new day, and that from that point forward things would be different. Then she put them in the same room together and demanded they bury the axe and commit to supporting each other. Under those circumstances, who doesn't say what their boss wants them to say? They both agreed to move forward together.

Lisa didn't physically wag her finger at her top performers, but she may as well have.

After the lecture, Lisa went back to trying to fix all of the process and execution issues that plagued her new team. But, six months later, she was still getting pulled into escalations where Jessica and Anil's teams were not working closely together. When Lisa addressed this, Jessica was quick to point out where Anil was letting her down. Anil, of course, had the same story.

Nothing had changed. The hatred remained, but had been swept under the rug. Lisa's attempt to clear the issue with a stern lecture had barely made a dent in the underlying team's mistrust of each other. In fact, when she dug deeper with her other employees, it slowly came to light that now Jessica and Anil had taken to lobbying outside of Lisa's division to get the division broken into two pieces so they didn't have to work together.

Keep the seven traits handy

Lisa's intent was right, but she got the calibration wrong. When faced with a detrimental inter-team situation, she didn't rely on her seven behaviors. She didn't get the facts. She didn't listen. She wasn't trying to be flexible. She wagged her finger, made a threat, and assumed things would get back on track.

What could she have done? She could have started by triangulating disputes outside of the parties involved. She could have listened carefully to ensure she was hearing what wasn't being said. Finally, she needed to make a judgment. Was the personality conflict something that could have been calibrated with a series of small actions? If so, she could have listed what those actions were and kept tabs on signs of success. If the personality

The 7 Behaviors of Great Middlers:

- *Focus on the Greater Good*
- *Seek Reality*
- *Commit to Listening*
- *Maintain Composure*
- *Display Courage*
- *Remain Flexible*
- *Act Decisively*

conflict had gone too far already, Lisa had a tougher decision to make and it was one that she wouldn't allow herself to consider: she was going to have to let one, possibly two, top performers go.

Luckily, Lisa didn't become successful by accident and she didn't have to make any cuts. In the end, she used her high emotional IQ and her flexibility to slowly rebuild trust between Jessica and Anil. It took longer than Lisa wanted it to, but her two A players (and their teams) finally began to display the behaviors of great middlers themselves. Success was not far behind.

The first calibration of the successful middler is ensuring that a team is cohesive and acting toward the same goals. Without this, nothing else matters. This can lead to tough decisions; ones that take all seven traits of great middlers, but none so much as the courage to act.

Inter-team Cohesion

The second calibration of great middlers is the outward facing team role of keeping more than one team working toward the same goal, balancing competing priorities and ensuring that the desired results are being cared for between the two teams.

The cross-functional governance committee

A close friend of mine, Jason, was asked to be the Support representative to a cross-functional governance committee at a large technology firm. This committee had multiple members, from marketing, legal and sales. But, most importantly, there was a member from the product side of the business and a member from support. These were the two most important members because they each represented roughly 50% of the company's total revenue.

The purpose of the committee was to align on long-term product direction and functions. As you can probably imagine, this could be a very contentious conversation. What's good for product sales (as determined by products or licenses sold) isn't always what's good for services (as determined by how often a support contract is attached to the product and then by how few calls support actually gets). So, Jason's job was to get product to agree to make product enhancements that reinforced more support contracts while making the actual number of support calls go down (Jason called this the product's 'serviceability.')

Product, on the other hand, wanted only to focus on those features that would entice customers to buy more product. And, with a limited budget, trade-offs needed to occur.

When Jason arrived on the scene, he found support merely did whatever product decided; the position on the governance committee that was granted to Support was really just to give Support organizations a 'heads up' on what was coming down the road.

Jason had a tough situation. His boss wanted more serviceability. But he knew that his counterpart's boss wanted more new features, not fixed old features. What was he to do?

Jason was a master of the seven traits. First and foremost, he was a diplomat who invested in relationships. He worked outside of the committee to socialize the importance of balancing features and serviceability. He brought facts to the table: before he joined the committee, the product division didn't even realize that support services made up 50% of the company's total profits, and over 60% of its margin. Jason arrived with the facts, invested in the relationships and made trade-offs with his counterparts in product. Although this often left his own boss a little miffed, Jason was able to bring results. Within a year, he had concrete evidence that serviceability features would be in the product version for the first time. And he could show that the most valuable of those had been prioritized first.

This is why Inter-team cohesion is the second calibration: if there's more than one team, and there almost always is, then you need the middle manager to ensure those teams know how to interact, when to interact and what the expected results are. Then, as always, get out of the way.

Top-Down Direction

Things change. Circumstances change. When you're a VP or higher, one of your primary jobs is to notice changes in the market, see coming trends and needs then get your team organized to take advantage of what's coming. This means perhaps changing direction on a product or moving into an adjacent market. It doesn't even need to be that dramatic. It could simply be changing economics means its time to tighten the belt on spending. Whatever the specifics, you need to not only get the message out you also need work to change. You need behaviors to change.

Enter the middler who is constantly looking up the chain of command for signals about changing direction or the need for changing behavior. Then, it's time to get to work: calibrate the team toward the new direction.

Bottom-up Direction

What goes for top-down direction also works the other way, or at least it does in great, high-functioning teams. When left to overcome challenges, innovate, and truly do outstanding work, ICs will often come across ideas or obstacles that need more than just themselves or their teams to move forward on. This is when good middlers will calibrate by taking that idea and pushing it both up the chain and across to other teams.

The lean-agile crackpot

At one of my previous posts, I ended up with a large development organization that was spreading all over the globe. At the time, the org was divided into about 10 different units, each with managers, who pretty much ran their teams as they saw fit. This led to some issues with reporting and the appropriate allocation of work across the entire team. I had been warned when I took over that there were budget and reporting issues. We needed clear line-of-sight for the entire year, across all teams and all functions.

Now, for most of the teams, this wasn't too big of a problem. They were already operating on an annual planning process and they would scope their projects down to every feature and function before the annual budget was fixed. Then they would start developing to that plan.

Of course, if they were already doing what I was being asked to go in and put in place, where was the disconnect? I had to dig deeper. So I decided to start with the one team that outright refused to operate like the other nine teams. The manager of that team had been referred to as the 'agile crackpot.'

If I was going to standardize anything, I might as well start with that one, right? So I went to the manager, Vijay, and started to gather my facts. I began with listening. Why did he do things the way he did? What was he trying to accomplish?

The Fallacy of the HIPPO

There's a new term I have come across: HIPPO management. This stands for the "Highest Important Person's Opinion." And it refers to the culture of most global companies that states decisions will be made based on the opinions of the most important person in the room.

No force has wrought more damage on the success of companies than HIPPO. None. Okay-- that is my opinion, and I can't back it up with any data. But the most successful new companies in the world make decisions based on data, not what leaders think should happen. Think of it as the "Moneyball-ization" of the modern world.

When applied to our topic here, the great middle manager must work with extra diligence to avoid being the HIPPO, and try to ensure his leaders are not leading by HIPPO either. This is where the fourth calibration comes into play: calibrating the endeavor from the bottom-up instead of the top down.

Vijay, it turned out, was a passionate innovator, not just from a technology perspective, but from a process perspective as well. He immediately pulled out two books that he urged me to read. He showed me the results he was getting with his agile process and how it differed from the other nine teams.

"The reason the other teams fail is because they backload risk to the end of projects," he told me. "We put our risk at the front. We discard failure as soon as possible instead of waiting for it to happen at the end of a huge, multi-year project."

Vijay had me back on my heels. He was speaking with so much rational thought, I had to stop what I thought my perceptions were and dig even deeper. So I read the books he suggested. I observed his team. And it absolutely changed my mind.

But that wasn't the hard part. Now, having seen what Vijay had accomplished, I needed to figure out not only how to get the other nine teams to do what Vijay was doing, but I needed to convince my boss (and his boss) that Vijay's approach, while flying in the face of their assumed logic of how the world worked, was the only thing that was going to save the organization and get our projects back on track.

In the end, I took a multi-stage approach. First, I brought in a 3rd party educator on the Lean-Agile development process for a three-day training seminar. Instead of inviting my team leaders to it, I invited business stakeholders and my boss to come and listen to the educator. He focused on the business benefits, how to leverage new business processes for greater development value, and armed these stakeholders with the metrics they should hold me and my team accountable to in a Lean-Agile world.

That worked beyond my best hopes. The business stakeholders were on-board and already talking about how they would 'hold my feet to the fire' to get better results. Gulp.

Next: moving Vijay's status with his peers from 'crackpot' to innovator. I went with a third party again, but instead of focusing on making anyone change their processes overnight, I spoke to how we would be tracking results and asked each of my managers to help me understand how they would be getting those results. This meant, at first, that I still had ten different processes, but at least I had a single set of measurements. Then, as new projects came in, we slowly began to institute new sets of tools. Pretty soon I was getting buy-in as lean-agile starting showing better results, and better relationships with our business stakeholders.

Not all the managers made it. Some simply could not transition to a new way of doing business and I had tough decisions to make. But within a single calendar year, I had a process that was 80% standard across the entire organization-- one that was located on three continents and in six different cities. And the other 20% I never tried to standardize. I knew that managers needed ways to tinker with their own processes to make them better.

You never know who the next crackpot will be.

Budget

It's true. Budgets can be very accurate and sometimes the budget at the start of the project is the same budget at the end. We say we will spend 100 dollars, and when we turn the receipt in, it's for 100 dollars.

But let's just go ahead and stare down the elephant in the room: the majority of time, the budget at the beginning of an endeavor is not the same one you end with. This isn't just in poorly run situations, either. It's just one of the challenges of a world of limited resources (or as I call it, "reality").

There are many different reasons for budget changes, but they typically have to do with changing priorities, a missed cost, timeline pressure or added sophistication.

It is the job of great middlers, be they project managers, line managers, or senior directors, is to pay attention to the changing landscape and make the necessary adjustments to the budget. Sometimes this means starving a poorly performing program or dumping available resources into a sensitive product that needs to hit the market sooner. Sometimes, this means keeping the right people informed of a budget requirement that wasn't visible at the onset of the endeavor.

Budget calibration can mean asking for more money. But it can also mean delivering the news to a team that budget has been tightened and other calibrations need to be made (scope, timeline, perhaps work-life balance). Great middle managers know how to employ the six traits of middle management to ensure these calibrations can be made while still caring for the other five.

Timelines and Deadlines

I've been in the software creation business, the customer service business and the virtual outsourcing business. My engagements and discussions with people in other lines of business have reinforced one of the primary lessons I've learned the hard way; no matter how ridiculous it is to ask when something will be done, the question will be asked and you must answer it.

Sometimes, the question makes sense and the variables are extremely well understood. You are doing a repeatable and oft-repeated task. You know who the resources on the team are and what they are capable of. So you can look at past performance, look at the requirements of the endeavor and you can come up with a reasonably accurate timeline.

Other times, this is not so easy. When I was in the database hero business, trying to get an utterly destroyed database back up and operational, the reason the database went down is often not known. The level of destruction is unclear. The steps required to get the data out could take 5 minutes or 5 days. But still, the first question from the VP on the call is: how long before the database is back up?

Doesn't matter how little you know. You have to answer the question. And a great middle manager will manage timelines and deadlines.

Sometimes this means managing expectations around when a timeline can be realistically drawn (the proverbial 'date when we will have the date'). Often it means breaking the news that, even though we had a reasonably accurate timeline, it no longer reflects reality. Whatever the case, great middle managers will remain firmly rooted in reality and care for the first five calibrations while managing a new timeline, a new deadline or managing the creation of them in the first place.

The Six Calibrations: the Really Hard Part

Taken individually, you could probably score yourself on a scale of 1-10 on how you perform in these six calibrations. You will come up with a few of them that you are great at and some that could use improvement. But here's the thing: to be great, you must care for all six simultaneously.

Granted, there are times when intra-team cohesion is more important than top-down direction, or budget changes will trump a timeline. But no matter what, when a great middle manager is calibrating, she is mindful of all these focus areas at the same time.

There is no other way to say it. If you want to be a really great middler, you have to consider how a calibration in one area will require an adjustment in another.

Furthermore, you will need to be practicing the six characteristics of great middle managers while you are doing all of this adjustment. If you lose site of the Greater Good, you may over-calibrate on team cohesion and over-rotate on the timeline. Without diplomacy, without top-shelf listening, you won't be able to judge the impact on a team of a particular budget change.

This is what it means to be a great middler: stand at the crossroads of competing demands and ensure the endeavor remains on track for success.

Chapter 4

The People in the Middle

When I talk about the middle, first and foremost I am referring to the work of the middle: the steadying hand and calibrating function required to achieve successful outcomes in complex endeavors. No matter how large or even how small, this work must be done.

In companies that have achieved a certain size, or are looking to grow, the middlework often becomes codified into particular job titles within the organization. This is middle management as typically categorized and identified in the wild. Much of the negative press about these roles will refer to middle management as a necessary evil, as something that technology can eliminate and that should be constantly flattened.

I'm not actually going to fight against those points of view. If your company does not want a job, don't make one. Everyone should leverage technology available to keep team members of all corporate levels closer to each other and with a finger on the pulse of organizational performance. Constantly looking to eliminate unnecessary roles is one of the jobs of a large and effective company.

However, middle work must get done. The calibration must be done to keep endeavors on track. Many times, middle work is done by middle management and I will argue that in many cases, this is for the best. In large enough endeavors, or complex projects, having a full-time calibration function is the glue that ensures success.

In this chapter, we will go through the typical middle management positions that are identified in companies and discuss their merits. I will end by discussing a few roles that are not often identified with middle management, but I have found to be the most critical middlers in a company.

Middle Management: Starting from the Bottom

When you look at the traditional literature, middle management is typically described as being above the line managers, or in other words, they are the managers of managers. I will get there in a moment, when I discuss that odd cat often referred to as the 'Senior Manager.' But because of my view of middle as a type of work, my view of middle management is more liberal, and includes anyone who manages people and is also managed. I do, however, exclude the "C Levels" – anyone with "Chief" in their title. While they do have a manager, the CEO, and they have very specific calibrating function, this book isn't about Chief Anything Officers (although I do hope they are reading this). I'll also discuss people who manage projects, and not necessarily people, as a particular form of middle manager later in this chapter.

But let's take a step back and move in a different direction. Let's start talking about middle roles where they typically start—in the delicate move from individual contributor to line manager.

Line Managers:
Middlers in the Trenches

We will spend more time with the transition from doer to calibrator in chapter 5. But it is worth pointing out that when we discuss the line manager, or field manager, often we are talking about a person that is managing others for the very first time and is in charge of sophisticated outcomes across a team instead of just his or her own output.

I can't overemphasize the importance of this transition or that it is necessary. Necessary in both senses: that the transition must take place and managers should be previous doers.

This can't always be the case—sometimes managers are previous managers, or come from different departments, different companies. But rarely in the real world do you get great middlers that start their careers in the middle. I'm not saying it doesn't happen. But cutting one's teeth in the business that you will later care for is the best training to understand the calibration functions one will own.

Typically, this person manages the doers of an organization, filing reports, managing performance, and seeing to the day-to-day needs of folks. It's easy to forget about the front line manager, or to assume it's a drone function, best performed by the happiest, albeit least intelligent, team member. But again: you need to be very careful. Bad line management is the downfall of many, many a great company.

I've seen this first-hand, on a large scale, and it's not pretty. An entire 3000 person organization and every line manager involved had no authority, no accountability, and no calibration skill. The work of the people that reported to them was measured at an automatic level by the workflow management system. If there was an issue, there was a separate escalation management process that flowed away from the line manager. Sure, they were responsible for their team's performance, but they had no way to influence it other than telling the team to focus more on the metrics. Which led to metrics gaming-- i.e., just shooting for the target that was provided and letting everything else go.

That company is insolvent now, for all kinds of reasons, but that was one of them. They had no idea what was happening at the actual level of execution.

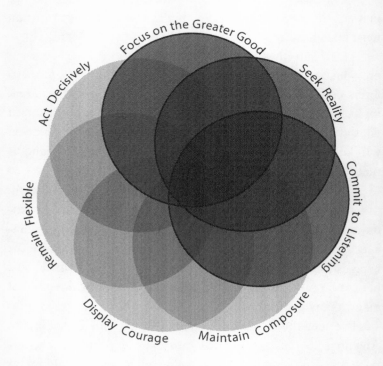

Line Manager: focus on Greater Good, Reality and Listening

While it remains true that any great middler displays all seven traits, a line manager will be best served by Focusing the Greater Good, Listening, and Seeking Reality.

Senior Managers: The Toughest Gig in the World

Most literature pegs the "middle management" moniker directly onto the role I refer to as the Senior Manager: the person buried below two or more layers above them and has at least one layer below. There is plenty of mirth to be had at the expense of the Senior Manager and not without cause; this layer can be the source of lots of body fat in a company.

Here's why: it's easier than you might think for this layer to simply disappear in the fabric of large to very large companies. With so many decisions being made above them and so much work being done below, what really does the Senior Manager do? They tell a small group of line managers to tell their people what to do, and they report up to someone that then reports up to someone else.

This problem is particularly noticeable (or, should I say, unnoticeable), in healthy, growing companies and industries. There's simply less at stake, and the Directors above the Senior Manager appreciates the way their guys make life easier. The managers below them may not appreciate their bosses all that much, but they don't mind. Besides that looks like the promise land. Line managers can't wait for their turn to get into that position.

As painful as they can potentially be, the senior manager role is nearly unavoidable, often invisible and rarely appreciated. This makes the Senior Manager job the toughest gig in the company—if you take yourself and your job seriously. Because the respect is hard to come by, and you will very often find yourself significantly bound on all sides with little room to influence outcomes as dramatically as you would like. So, you settle into the role and disappear, or you fight tooth and nail to get moved up ever so incrementally into a Directorship someplace, where you can really drive value.

Here is how I've seen great middlers succeed at the Senior Management job: when they are used sparingly. If there are too many Senior Managers then a company is probably not getting its money's worth. In fact, I would argue that you may need close to as many Directors as you have Senior Managers. The pyramid of the corporate ladder straightens out at this rung. I know good leaders who struggle to differentiate between Directors and Senior Managers because of this. Admittedly, when you go to the nebulous 'middle of the middle' role, accountability and focus get harder to define.

Senior Managers need a different behavior intensity than a line manager. They are maturing, seeing more of the playing field, and so inter-team calibration takes on a larger role than intra-team dynamics. He may not be setting direction, like a Director or VP, and so does not have accountability for big directional decisions. But he is exposed to more of the top-level decision making and thinking and sees the competing priorities more clearly. More diplomacy, more greater good.

The facts are going to get murkier. They are being filtered on both ends, both coming down from above and bubbling up from below. Listening is important, but staying rooted in reality becomes more difficult.

Great Senior Managers have a clear understanding of just how deeply in the middle they are and see that as a strength.

Being a strong conduit of both energy and information is the top priority and adherence to the Greater Good is critical. If the Senior Managers don't internalize what's important for a company, the company is in big trouble.

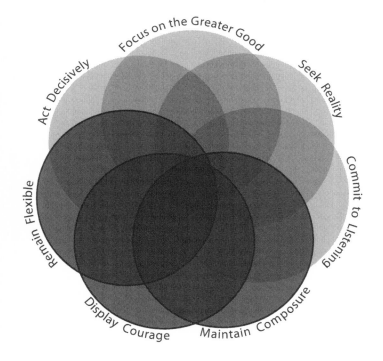

Senior Manager: focus on Composure, Flexibility and Courage

Middle Management:
Near the top

While they look less like middle management from TV shows like "The Office," managers who are near the top of the corporate ladder have middle work to do. The behavior intensity patterns must emphasize different traits at this altitude to be successful.

Directors

I like the title "Director." That's a cool name. I remember the first time I was promoted to be a Director and received my business cards. Director. I recorded my voicemail greeting.

"This is Matt Hart, Director of Whatever Important Thing…"

Nice. It sounds good, doesn't it? I'm not just managing anymore. I'm directing. Like in the movies. I am pointing at how to get things done.

These are nice fantasies, albeit partially true. But the director still must calibrate up and down, although the calibrations have far more influence than they did at the lower levels. There's an amplification effect the more power a person has in terms of moving people.

But I call it a fantasy for a reason. After being a Director for a month, I quickly came to the realization that more than ever before, I needed to focus on calibrating the endeavor toward success. Suddenly, I was responsible for a multi-million dollar budget with an even larger value to the company. To keep this organization on the right track, spending money in the right places, cost cutting in the right places, while keeping my eye on the Greater Good—it was just getting harder and harder.

I found being a director the most gratifying of any position I've held at a company; but it also took more energy, more focus and more calibration than any other. Great middle managers at the director level must be able to put themselves in the shoes of the calibrators they manage without losing sight of the (much) bigger picture.

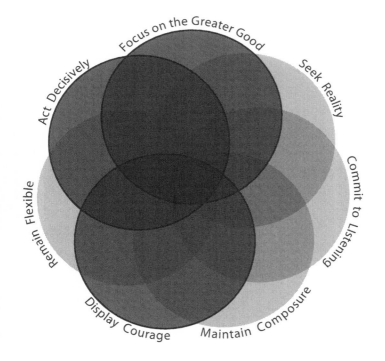

Director: focus on courage, decisiveness, and the Greater Good

When it comes to the behaviors of a Director, the focus must move to Courage, Decisiveness and a strong view of the Greater

Good. At this level, if there is no commitment to the endeavor, you will see big problems in the overall team dynamics.

Vice Presidents:
Kings of the Middle

There's a good argument that at the VP level, we are talking more about leadership, vision, setting direction and watching out for massive trends. And you would be right. In great companies, Vice Presidents are spending time with Presidents and Chief Officers, watching the market closely and managing directives and outcomes.

But there's another side of being a Vice President. When I speak with them privately, they often talk about the same kinds of pressures and activities that are associated with lower-level employees: calibrating top-down directives, finding ways to bring messages from within their groups up to the level of visibility to effect change and ensuring team cohesion. In other words, they are spending a lot of time and energy doing middlework.

Moreover, when asked to describe what makes a good Vice President, many of the same behaviors appear that we've discussed in this book; they have a strong handle on the conflicting priorities that drive the company (they Focus on the Greater Good), they stay devoted to the facts (they Seek Reality) and they are Display Courageous. The behavior intensity diagram looks very different for the Vice President than it does for others. As we discussed in chapter two, you see a different behavior pattern with each concentric circle of responsibility. However, the more influence a middler has, the more all seven traits become critical.

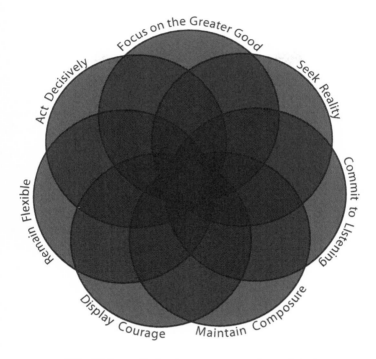

VP: All Seven Behaviors, strong and consistent

In addition to the behaviors they display, they also take on the calibration activities of the middle, albeit not as their full-time gig usually. But when polled, VPs will tell you that they are responding to budget changes, timeline adjustments, managing information up and down and ensuring teams work well together.

This is why I often refer to Vice Presidents as the "Kings of the Middle." This is where really, really good middlers find themselves—sometimes by choice, other times because they are simply needed there.

The "P" Managers: The most important middle work in your company

I have spent time so far in this chapter discussing middle managers in the more traditional sense: people who are bosses of other people in the most direct way. They show up as the boss in organizational structure diagrams, they manage human resource issues, fill out performance reviews and make final decisions on raises, bonuses and firings.

However, there are three other roles that I want to speak to, not just to be collectively exhaustive, but also because my analysis has shown that these folks may just be the most critical members of any endeavor and we rarely speak of them. When we do, we typically destroy them or pity them. They get in our way, pester us for updates, set up meetings, push for reports, and in so many other ways make a nuisance of themselves. Who are they?

The Project Managers

I have a close friend, Pratham, who runs an outsourcing company in India, and we came up through the ranks together at a previous company. His career started in the software development organization as a coder, and he was really, really good at this. He made many impressive things and in general is a lot smarter than I am. When we finally came into contact and worked on some projects, he was a front-line manager and I was a Senior Manager within a software development team. We had a lot of aggressive goals and we had a project manager assigned. At first I was overjoyed—this would really help! But my friend just shook his head in disgust.

"Just watch, Matt," Pratham said in his quiet voice. "We will have to get things done in spite of the PM. They are all bums."

Boy, was he right. The project managers at this company had gone the route of many a good project management team in global corporations: they saw themselves as mere information handlers, passing data from one person to the other, managing spreadsheets and accepting information handed to them without even the smallest of analysis.

It was a cultural issue, and I don't blame the people doing the work necessarily. But the PM assigned to help my team get our work done merely called meetings, asked for updates, consolidated those updates and then sent out an update.

In the end, Pratham and I ended up moving the project manager out of the team and assigning accountability to the line managers in charge of development. The middlework still had to be done; but in this case, we felt we had better middle behaviors from the direct managers.

Great Project Management and Avoiding the Secretary Trap

I've known and run the Project Management Office at two different companies. A great one will propel you forward; a bad one will do nothing. Literally, it won't hurt you too much, just burn through budget.

Here's the secret truth behind so many project management offices in large companies: it's a way for individual contributors and line managers, product and portfolio managers, to get the one thing that they all want but can't afford: a secretary.

The line is tough to draw, but it's there: an admin schedules meetings, catering, creates the PowerPoint presentations, takes orders and fulfills orders. And in many cases, this is all a Project Manager is asked to do.

So what does a great project manager do? He may perform the clerical tasks—they do have to get done, and if you can afford to move that out of the IC's hands, that's great. But if that's all they do, call it what it is: a shared admin that you don't have to tell the executives about. But a great project manager, well, a great one displays the seven behaviors we discussed in chapter 2. And the toughest ones for a PM? Displaying Courage and Acting Decisively.. Because the Project Manager is responsible for keeping a team on track, but isn't anyone's boss, it takes real courage to stand up to the members of the team and demand the facts, synthesize them, and make tough judgments on calibrating budget or timelines.

The Program Manager

Sometimes used interchangeably with the Project Manager, the Program Manager oversees a series of interconnected projects. Calling someone a program manager is a way to differentiate a level of competence and complexity. In extremely large endeavors, you may have a number of project managers that are accountable to a program manager.

Unfortunately, I've personally made a mockery of these titles, and probably ushered in part of the problem at least at one company. In that case, I had someone who was a project manager but was hungry for personal advancement and recognition. What did I do? Promoted them to program manager. Did the actual work change? Nope. New title. These empty titles are like grade inflation in our schools: they don't make anyone better; they make them worse.

A great program manager is capable of managing a larger, more complex set of interconnected endeavors without losing site of the calibrations required without losing their footing in reality, in ensuring facts are gathered and collected and that objective decision-making is facilitated.

Product Manager

The Product Manager is a strange beast and one that is often confused with a project manager. This is a shame, as they are not the same role, not the same job and do not have the same responsibilities. They are both, of course, middlework, and therefore have a calibrating function. This is probably why Project and Product Managers are often confused (along with the clearly similar name).

But a Product Manager stands at the middle of a much larger intersection of interests and needs. A great product manager must be intimately familiar with the customers of the company and the industry itself. But they must also know the company's Greater Good and remain dedicated to it. They need a great working knowledge of how the product they manage is built, organized and sold. Sometimes they will oversee the work of multiple project managers while trying to get their product out the door.

The Product Manager is the most middle of any person in an organization. And the most important because of it. This is ultimate act of middlework calibration: budgets, timelines, teamwork, sales teams, customers, executives. Sooner or later, they all want a piece of the product manager.

Boy, have I seen some bad ones. I would argue that I watched a great company, with great technology, slowly waste away and

Corporate Title Grade Inflation

Assigning new titles to recognize a capable person without actually changing their accountability (or even the pay grade, for that matter) isn't unique to the project manager role. This happens throughout companies at all levels. I myself have been made a Senior Director from a Director, even as my accountability and authority shrunk.

I typically advocate against this purely on principle: titles should reflect the reality of authority, influence, and scope. But it's a tough call, particularly in stagnant or shrinking companies where scope will not typically keep up with great people's ambitions. To keep a resource, you will want to recognize the contribution in a way. And to those looking for promotion, they are interested in seeing the better title even if it's just so they can put it on their resumes and LinkedIn profiles.

In other words, title inflation comes from a genuine need. But it can be very harmful to a company. You will find yourself in mature companies with hundreds of VPs, many of whom haven't changed the work they do in years, but simply been given bigger and bigger titles. This actually can make these great resources vulnerable from an 'optics' perspective: it looks like the company is 'top heavy' with 'too many executives.' When the knives come out to carve away at perceived corporate largesse, these executives are at risk.

Promoting great resources is important. But I've come to the realization over the past two decades that rewarding these resources with greater accountability, more challenging problems and better opportunities will get you farther than simply giving them a new title.

die because the product managers gave up calibrating.

Great product management is something to behold; I wish every company understood the importance of it, invested it in, and developed it as a strong practice within their ranks.

Organizational Structure: A Primer

No conversation of different roles and management layers can avoid the question: what SHOULD a great company look like? How many layers of management are the right number? What should the span of control look like? How can I tell if I have an unhealthy middle?

When you talk to health and fitness experts, they will tell you this: body fat moves to the weakest parts of the body. In other words, you can be a great cyclist and have extremely fit legs, but still carry a spare tire around your gut.

This is a good metaphor when looking at the health of an organization, particularly the middle parts. You need good core muscles, but it's easy for fat to stick around your belly and back because you are focusing on your arms and legs. If you want to know if you have a healthy middle, look for the fat.

There are four dimensions to consider when you decide it's time to take a good hard look at how an organization is structured. These four elements exist whether you are talking about a group of 4 employees or 400. Let's look at each of them separately.

1. People

The first dimension you need to understand is people. Who currently works in this function? How many? Where are they?

What are their skills, backgrounds, future plans, projects?

To get this information laid out correctly, it's critical to explore how the people are organized. This means getting the org chart. Yes, but you need to dig deeper than just the structure of who reports to whom. In addition, you need to see where people are actually working-- what team structure exists? Do people get their work, and report back on that work, to the person that they report to? Or does work report through a different structure in a matrixed fashion?

2. Process

What are the business processes that this organization supports and which business processes do they use (or consume)? This discovery process is best facilitated, in my opinion, by the tools offered by Lean or Six Sigma methodologies. These schools of thought are too vast a topic for this book, but they provide a way to map what a process is, end to end, and then identify where the biggest inefficiencies exist at every step or hand-off. This waste identification can be informal within a team or it can be a formal engagement (often known as a Kaizen event).

3. Function

You may notice that in identifying the four dimensions, what is absent is discovering what people are actually working on. That is intentional for two reasons. First, people will tell you what they are doing. When you start probing, people are quick to bring their work to the surface. Second, focusing on the work doesn't get you to the heart of the matter.

What you need to focus on first is understanding the business functions being served by the organization. Make a complete list, and here's the hard part, you have to be brutally honest. Don't start by listing the business processes the team should be performing. Nope. Start with the real. We'll get to the ideal state in a minute.

Getting to the real gets back to the core behaviors: seek the facts, and commit to listening. For instance, if you are looking at the functions of a project management office, don't just listen for what the project managers are telling you they do. Instead, ask the team members as well. In one case where I was performing a culture transformation, I found that the Project Managers were, in fact, performing all the HR duties typically associated with someone's boss. You must dive deeper, and listen carefully, to get the real 'lay of the land.'

4. Technology (tools)

Finally, you need to understand what tools are facilitating the functions, processes and people. This is important because you can unearth ways to improve productivity, but just as importantly, you will unearth functions that you may not realize are being performed when you look at the tools.

The four dimensions: mapping the current state to the steady state

Once you have your head wrapped around the current state along our four dimensions, it's time to decide what you want it to look like in the optimal steady state. There could be all kinds of factors that weigh on this. Perhaps you need to cut costs. Perhaps you need to expand the scope of work. Perhaps there is a wider initiative to consolidate technology tools.

Whatever the constraints, you need to make a list before you define the steady state. This isn't an ideal utopia; it's a look at what you can realistically accomplish. Then define what the steady state looks like for each of the four dimensions.

	Current State	End State
People		
Process		
Function		
Tools		

The Four Dimensions of Transformation: Current and Steady State

You should have two columns now: current state and steady state. What is different? What will need to change? Now you have your delta. Now you know what you need to get done.

Set a timeline, plateaus, and measures

You need to understand how long the change will take to get from where you are today to the steady state across all four dimensions. I've found it to be critically important to set plateaus up along the way. What will each dimension look like in 3 months? 6 months? 9 months? All the way until you get to the steady state. These plateaus give you a way to assess how you are doing.

What you will notice immediately when you try to set plateaus is that you need measures to see how you are doing. There is no way to know you are getting to the steady state unless you can measure progress.

Measuring progress needs to focus on measuring the results of the change, not just the activity in change. I consulted on a transformation of a Lab Management team at global company and the leader in charge of implementing the changes kept identifying activities to measure at each plateau. For instance, one of the results the company was looking to improve was the time-to-completion of lab setup for new development projects. To be more effective at this, the lab manager needed to put a ticketing and tracking tool in place. That was put as a measure: ticketing system installed and in use.

	Current State	3 Months	6 months	End State
People				
Process				
Function				
Tools				

The Four Dimensions: Building Plateaus and Measuring Progress

Wrong answer. While the ticketing system was vitally important, the real measure is the time-to-completion. That is the result to measure; the ticketing system was a project that needed to be done to support it.

Organizational Structure: People in the Middle

Yes, I have opinions on how to structure the middles of organizations; but it's worth pointing out I've always been in high tech companies or in IT departments. There are always parallels and it's worth exploring where the patterns emerge in terms of how to maximize the value of the middle of a company. That exploration begins with a look at how to structure the work management.

Decide if your people managers are your work managers

To an individual contributor, the two scariest words in big corporations are: Matrix Management. For the uninitiated, matrix management is when you have someone that you report to directly, who is actually your boss and cares for your HR needs and concerns, but does not actually assign or judge the work you do.

For the worker, the way to interpret this structure is with this question I was once asked when I was implementing a matrix:

"Wait, the guy who determines my bonus isn't the same guy that tells me what to work on?"

The following diagram shows a picture of how matrix management looks like and operates.

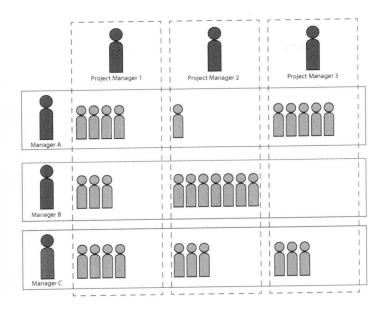

Matrix Management in Action

Matrix management can work and can work extremely well. Matrix management keeps the overall span of control low, allowing for a relatively flat organization. People managers have as their primary goal the calibrating activities associated with keeping people happy and engaged, team disputes resolved and the like.

But this only works with great "P" managers. If the project, program and product managers are not courageous strong leaders, then matrix management will fail. Workers will not be able to tell that the project manager is accurately reflecting their contributions to the people manager and vice versa.

So, when you are building a high-functioning middle layer,

consider the strength and presence of the P's that will be doing work allocation before you decide on a matrix structure. If it's not there, figure out if it's in your sphere of influence to change. If not, keep work and people managers the same.

The danger in people managers and work managers being the same is it can create a conflict of interest. Here's how that happens. Let's say Jan is a line manager and she has 10 software developers that work for her. She is, herself, judged by how well those developers work: how much did they get done, how fast they get it done and how much value the software they develop produces. All fine. So, Jan gets assigned a project. But the project only requires 8 people to work on it. Now what?

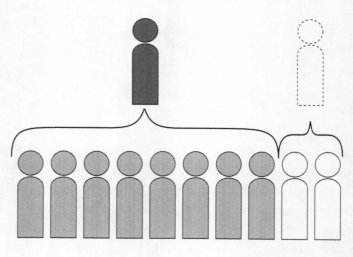

Jan loans two resources to another manager

Sure, Jan could seek other projects to either work on herself, or she could "loan out" the two free resources. But now, you have two people working in an informal matrix structure already-- but not all 10. Furthermore, Jan may look at her project and think, I want to create some slack so I can really succeed and over-deliver on my primary project. So, she keeps all 10, even though the project may not require that.

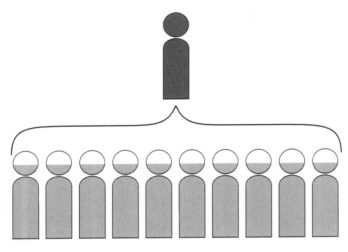

Jan keeps all resources who are all under-utilized

But wait, there's more. Let's say that two people do get loaned to a different project. Now, it comes time for annual performance review. Jan needs to reward people, but she is naturally predisposed to reward those that made her project, and her own performance evaluation, go so well. Those two resources on loan are extremely concerned that they are getting overlooked and will lobby to stay put and not be loaned out.

An even more concerning situation can emerge: a change in corporate direction occurs and a new project is put into place after Jan and all her peers have already taken on projects and their teams are hard at work. How does this project get slotted in? Will Jan offer to slow her delivery down and put five of her resources on a new project that may be more important for the company but not gain her any recognition on the project that will determine her fate?

These conflicts of interest can be overcome with great middle managers demonstrating the seven behaviors and staying focused on the six calibrations. But you can also structurally help everyone stay as agile and flexible as possible with the right structure. It's why when I'm given the opportunity to structure large-scale execution teams, I work toward a matrix organization and over-spend on getting great middle managers to run it.

Determining span of control

"Span of control" is typically the corporate term for how many people report to each manager in the org chart. If I am a Director, how many Senior Managers do I have? And how many Managers report in to each Senior Manager?

There is no right size for span of control. Everyone who gives you a rule of thumb is doing so only because they have an ulterior motive that needs to be satisfied. Often, there are HR and corporate directives that give manager-to-IC ratios that directors and VPs are judged against. This is the worst kind of corporate behavior. If you are forced to follow these arbitrary guidelines, you can work to try and change the policy, or you can just follow it, but it represents as lazy a metric of corporate performance as there is. Having said that, things can get too flat in my experience. When a middler is truly caring for inter-team and intra-team calibrations, having more than 15-16 direct reports probably means someone is getting missed or taking advantage of the anonymity.

Gauge the level of non-personnel related work that is required by a position and how much work ownership is being levied on the manager. If their role is to just manage people (work is matrixed), then load them up and keep the organization flat. If there are work ownership requirements and HR components, then something will get dropped if the span goes to high.

The bottom line is that you can look at the number of layers and find if there is fat that needs trimming. If one person has two directs, who has two directs, who has two directs... something is probably wrong unless you are incubating Future leaders.

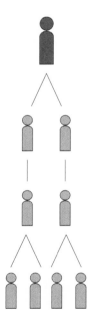

Questionable org structure: tall and thin

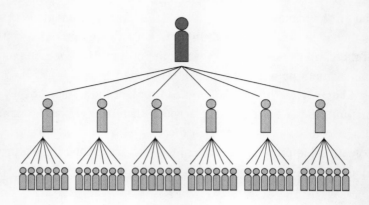

Healthy org structure: wide and flat

The final advice I would give is follow the four dimensional process of discovery and change. By diving into these areas, you will come to see clearly what management structure the situation calls for. But if you create a management structure before you know where you want to go, operationally, you will be fighting the wrong battles at the wrong times.

Chapter 5

Get to the Middle and Make it Better

Early on in my conversations as a manager and organization transformer, I would get asked by the doers, who are equal parts curious and ambitious, what does it take to move into management? What can I do to start my walk up the corporate ladder?

Over the years, I've change my tune pretty dramatically on this subject as I've come into more and more contact with both great and horrible middlers. As has been pointed out in the literature many times, a great engineer does not make a great manager. Being good at your job doesn't mean you will be good at managing people doing that job.

I have put together a set of behaviors and activities to make this transition more effective and more valuable, both to the individuals seeking to move into the middle and to the companies that need a great middle.

Set the stage

First, you need to check on yourself and your long-term goals. That is a topic for another book. Let's assume at this point

---

Transition to the Middle: How to Get There

- *Set the stage*
- *Eliminate entitlement*
- *Get your head out of the (IC) sand*
- *Act the part before you have the part*
- *State your intentions*
- *Do the work before you get paid for the work*
- *Strive for networking and visibility*
- *Treat the role with respect*

---

you've checked in with your five year plan, your spouse and possibly your life coach and you've decided: heading up the corporate ladder is for you. You want to move from being a doer to a middler. This decision should not be either the default choice or taken lightly. Middlework is not for everyone.

Perhaps you want to move all the way up to the top. I admire your ambition and we'll talk about that at the end of this chapter (Moving Through the Middle). Maybe you just feel your calling is to play a larger role in a successful endeavor. Perhaps you have watched for a while as a middle manager at some level has struggled mightily and endeavors have failed. Whatever the motivation, you want to move on.

Great. Congratulations. So the first step is to check your pride at the door.

Eliminate entitlement

In chapter 2, I equated flexibility with humility and emphasized the importance of not assuming you know what is right, what

Call to Action, Leaders: Make an IC Career Path

This is a great place to make a plea to the org structure gurus and HR departments of the world: ensure your company has a career and promotion path other than management and middle-work.

Too much damage to productivity, people's careers, and the general stress level of companies is done simply because the only way to improve oneself at a company is by joining the management ranks. This can be crippling to a company particularly in the high-tech industry I come from. Having invested time and money in a great engineer, you force that engineer to leave work she loves because there's only one way to move up.

By taking the time to think through what an increasingly larger role, accountabilities and authority should come within an IC's role, you can ensure that you keep great minds doing what great minds do and not force a square peg into a round hole.

This also serves as a reminder to every worker who feels compelled to move into management: there are other ways! For instance, many technology companies have a "Technical Career Ladder" defined. It shows how to progress from a software developer to senior software developer, to software architect, to software director, to software fellow. At each step, the role and influence grows both inside the company and in the larger industry. Before you jump into that Program Manager role that looks so tempting, talk to HR. See what you can do within your competency.

Looking through the Crack in the Door

At any level in the company, you get a view of what is happening around you. You come to understand the pressures, the trade-offs, and machinations that are keeping the endeavor moving. But there is a danger in getting the glimpse you have, particularly at the IC level. This is the "Crack in the Door" Dilemma.

Imagine you are walking down a hallway and you hear a commotion in a room. You stop and notice a door which is open just a few inches. You glance in and you see someone shouting in an angry voice. You can't make out what he is saying, but you can tell that it's not good.

What do you know of the situation? Can you interpret it? Who is he mad at? What is he yelling about? Let's say you know this person, and you talked to him earlier in the day, and he expressed his frustration at something. Is that what he is angry about in the room?

If you jump to conclusions, you might get it right. But you don't know what else is happening in the room. Who else is in there?

I give this example because we often believe we understand the motivations and mechanisms for why a leader is acting a certain way, but we don't. We don't understand what she is trying to calibrate. We may not be able to see across to different teams and understand the needs and issues across the same scale.

So, before you jump to any conclusions, make sure you have as many facts as you can gather, and always remember: you only have a small crack to look through. Don't assume you know what is happening in there.

will work or who is the best. As an Individual Contributor, you may be the very best at your job. Perhaps you are already performing tasks that a middle manager should be doing.

If you want to be great in the middle, however, you have to eliminate entitlement from your attitude and mindset. You don't deserve anything.

That requires saying again: you don't deserve anything. If you want to move up into middle management, whether that's from an IC role to a manager or from a manager to the next level, you cannot start from a place where you believe you are entitled to the promotion.

Every day in the world is basically a reboot. You earn your keep every day. And you must prove yourself through and through to first get, then retain, and then succeed at middle management roles.

Get your head out of the sand

This piece of advice is the corollary to the entitlement rule. My experience has always shown that the other side of the entitlement coin is a healthy dose of self-delusion about one's self-worth. Again, humility will be your best friend in this process. You don't have to pretend that you suck at everything. Just don't delude yourself.

The habit of keeping your eyes open starts with actively beginning to pay attention to what is happening around you. What roles are people playing? What are people saying about the work? Are people happy?

And—here's the hard part—this extends beyond the team you work on. Do you have visibility into other parts of the company? What is going on over there? As I'll introduce later in this chapter, you need to begin to build a fabric of people you know throughout the organization. This starts by paying attention.

You need to begin to see beyond the deliverables and see how sophisticated endeavors take place. Watch this in your company, but also start to ask into how it happens elsewhere. Join professional communities. Attend conferences.

Get your head out of the sand.

Act the part before you have the part

So, you're practicing active humility—earning your keep every day without entitlement. You are keeping your head out of the sand, paying attention to how teams are interacting and how overall work is being coordinated and calibrated. Great.

Now for the challenge: start acting the part before you have the part. You should begin this process before you state your intentions. This is because of a very simple universal truth in large companies: it's easy to promote someone into a role you are confident they can perform. It's much harder to take a chance on someone who you have never seen perform the activities of that role.

To get to the point where you can prove you are capable of doing the work, you first have to act the part. That means demonstrating the seven behaviors of great middle managers. Because these behaviors don't necessitate a middle position to practice and habituate, you can start doing this anytime. The same can be said for the six calibrating activities; you can begin working on team cohesion and managing messages before it is your paid job to do so.

Because you have already eliminated entitlement, you are working on your flexibility. You have pulled your head out of the sand, so you immediately start practicing Knowing the Greater Good and staying Firmly Grounded in Reality. That's a lot of the battle. Start practicing your listening, your diplomacy, and flexing your courage muscles in small ways to build up the habits.

This will get you, your peers and your boss ready for the next step.

State your intentions

This may seem obvious, but it is actually more difficult—and more dangerous—than many people let on. First is the difficult part, actually stating out loud to your current manager that you are interested in moving into the middle. To do so, you have to ensure you know what you mean. You are coming from a humble place, but you have confidence that you can make a difference at the next level. This needs to get communicated. Second, you need to articulate your willingness to be patient, but that you are ready now. Third, you are willing to put in the effort to attain the new level.

Stating your intentions and having it surprise a manager won't get you very far; that's the dangerous part. It can be seen as intimidating or, worse, as a sign that you are disgruntled and looking to leave. But if you have been practicing the middle behaviors, this desire will not necessarily surprise them. They may have reservations, but that's when the next step comes into play.

Do the work before you get paid for the work

Offer to take on small steps and projects that will further provide experience. Yes, you are doing work that you are not getting paid for. And, chances are, you will not be allowed to take something else off your plate.

Get over it. If you want the return, you have to invest. In this case, you are investing in a dramatic change in your job profile and long-term career. So keep your grousing to yourself and dive in to the get the work done.

What kind of work? It could be managing a special project. It could be acting in a team-lead role to run a series of meetings and small sub-projects. It could be working to get an obstacle removed. Whatever the task, you can be guaranteed that it's something that your manager needs done and doesn't have time to do. It may not seem that important. But understand one thing: by taking this on, you have achieved one of the hardest accomplishments in global corporations, getting on-the-job training. Never miss an opportunity for OJT. Remember I said that.

Strive for Networking and Visibility

When you consider taking on a special project, or stating your intention to move into the middle, you need to account for two primary components of success as a middler: your personal network and your visibility. These are two sides of the same coin, but need to be cared for in slightly different ways.

Networking

Networking in this context refers to the act of making new connections with other people and then sustaining them. This is an important definition, particularly if you are an introvert or just starting out on your career. First, you need to actively put your-

The Virtual Networking Job

You can successfully create and sustain networks without face-to-face time, as implied in this book. I've been working from home for years, and many of the best middle managers are responsible for teams or work all over the globe. To successfully network without having to travel all over the place, you need to focus on your communication tools: Have a good headset. A quiet room. Be ready for a videoconference at any time (ie, don't dress in your pajamas all day if you work from home). Utilize instant messaging to sustain conversations and make small talk when you are on a conference call. The important thing is to take the extra time to create networking opportunities when they aren't readily apparent.

self in positions to meet people. And when we say, meet people, this can mean any situation where you are shaking hands and taking names of people you didn't already know.

As a lifelong introvert, networking is the toughest thing for me to achieve. I'm perfectly happy networking with characters in fictional books, but when it comes to meeting and remembering the names of actual people, I'm not exactly the best. You either know this from experience or have seen people like me.: They show up at a party with a person and spend the entire party talking to that one person.

You also know that other type; the one that appears magical to me. She walks into a party and immediately begins systematically working the crowd, talking to as many people as she can.

These are the extremes. If you naturally move around a

room like the latter, then you can skip the rest of this section. But if you struggle to make connections, here are a few steps you can take to get better at it. And this is not just for the purposes of work, although we will focus on a professional setting for the sake of the book.

Prepare to Network

> "In preparing for battle I have always found that plans are useless, but planning is indispensable."
> -- Dwight D. Eisenhower

The first step is to be prepared to network. The biggest mistake I always make is this one: I get to a networking event or opportunity. I start having a great conversation. The other person asks for my card. Sure, no problem...

I forgot my business cards.

Make sure you consciously consider the responsibility you have to yourself to be ready for any networking opportunity that might come up. Have your business cards. Have your elevator pitch. Be ready before the opportunity comes.

Take names and follow up immediately.

When you are in networking situations, do one thing if you do nothing else: find a way to remember names. If you get a card, take the time to flip it over and write a few key words when you get a chance. But get and remember names.

If there was an interesting conversation or possible follow up implied, take the action as soon as possible. Don't let a few weeks go by. Take the time to send an email or make a follow up call within a few days.

Sustaining relationships

Getting into the world and meeting people isn't enough by itself. You also need to put energy into sustaining relationships. This step is less obvious, but equally important. How do you keep relationships with people?

In the workplace this is less difficult. Projects pull you together. The workplace pulls you together. But outside of that, you need to deploy methods both old and new to keep yourself in touch and connected. There are old-fashioned methods: follow up calls, follow up emails, invitations to lunch. Then there are new ways: follow on twitter or on LinkedIn.

What About Facebook?

The fact is, people may not want you to be their 'friend.' They post pictures of their kids, argue about gun control, and basically try to have a life. It's not a professional networking platform, and frankly, I think its sort of rude to reach out to colleagues or new connections in that form. Perhaps over time, the relationship can grow. Until then, stick with Twitter and LinkedIn. These platforms are better suited to professional relationships, and more often used for professional networking.

Professional Visibility

When I talk about visibility, I am referring to the ability of those around you in all directions (peers, superiors, and even your current employees) to be able to identify and have an opinion about the quality of your work. This is a critical component of finding mobility in any direction at medium to large companies. There is simply too much going on to expect people to take an active interest.

Visibility from your current boss or workgroup is probably going to happen naturally. But that's not visibility, per se; those folks have an active need for their own jobs and livelihoods to know what you're up to, how you perform and if you are reliable or not. But to take your career into the middle, you need people beyond that circle to vouch for you.

How do you get this visibility? Networking is the first step, which we discussed previously. Taking on additional projects helps too, but here is where you need to be selective about types of projects. You specifically need ones that have impacts, touch-points and dependencies outside of your immediate circle. Without that, you may not be getting the right visibility.

Treat the role with respect

Remember all the effort, all the schooling, all the hunting you did in order to land your first job? You spent years in classes. Later you built a pedigree of on-the-job training. All of that paid off and you found work that you've been mastering ever since.

So it's time to ask you: how much effort have you put into becoming a manager? Chances are, you haven't spent even a fraction of the time and energy into it as you did making your first career choice.

And that's fine. You will be leveraging what you've learned as an IC to become a great middler. But you need to treat the role with respect and understand that it requires a different set of skills and capabilities from what you've done so far. So put in some training. Find the seminars, internal opportunities and personal experiences that you can use to develop the skills.

Remember why you got into the business in the first place

One final note on the subject of getting to the middle: being a middler isn't about getting to the middle, really. It's about what being in the middle can do for the endeavor you are a part of. So remember what got you into your line of work in the first place. Keep that at the front of your mind. That's why you are there; and it's why you are going to make the middle better.

Building a Better Middle

In chapter 2 we discussed the seven behaviors that you need to practice every day in order to be an excellent middle worker. Then we focused in on the six calibrations in chapter 3. When it comes down to it, by focusing on the those chapters, it has been my experience that you will not only succeed yourself, but you will be doing what is most required of someone in the middle.

There are a few final notes on specific things you can do to strengthen the middle you occupy; to make not only yourself better, but those around you. By taking just a few extra steps you can help transform the experience of those around you.

Know the work of those that you manage

Moving into middle management is not an excuse to stop learning or caring about the actual work of the doers. You should be investing time and energy in remaining somewhat current on the type of activities and results expected of people in your workgroups.

You will get rusty. Don't expect to keep up with those doing what they do all day. But it is critical to keep a skill in your toolkit other than management, even if you are not the best at it.

Keep your street cred

One of the toughest balancing acts in the middle is delivering tough messages from above without alienating the folks who work for you. Here's why: you don't gain any credibility by rejecting the message itself. A lot of middle managers use language like this:

Yeah, those jerks over finance just cut the budget again. Can you believe those guys?

I'm just as much a victim of this as you are.

I don't want to have to tell you this.

Using this kind of language means you are not doing the calibrating and filtering work required. You are chickening out. In other words, it's the worst kind of behavior. Even if all of those statements feel true, you must resist. They don't help keep the endeavor on track—they just make your job as a manager easier. But the truth is if that's all you are going to say, your boss doesn't need you. You are just passing the message along unedited and even with color commentary that hurts the situation.

Even more importantly, you actually lose loyalty and credibility. You come across looking like a patsy who doesn't have an opinion.

Maintaining street credibility is important. But you don't get it by throwing the execs under the bus. Instead, you get it by connecting the tough messages with what the team is doing. By showing courage when you disagree with the message. Take the following examples:

I heard about the cut, and I pushed back on the Director, asking if there was a different way for us to save that money. We looked at travel, we looked at new laptops, but in the end, this is the only way to keep this project on track.

When I pressed the Director, he gave me a few alternatives. I agree that this is the best one.

I pressed the Director to take this to the team and see if anyone could help us brainstorm a better approach. Any ideas?

Stay out of the way

This is always easier to say than do, but great middle managers work every day to stay out of the way of their reports. This is a discipline that needs constant attention. It can be way too easy to schedule another meeting or demand another type of progress report when your boss changes his mind or changes the dynamic. Sending a series of emails asking for an update by the end of day means you are creating interruptions that stop the flow of execution.

A great middle manager works hard to avoid standing in the way of work getting done in an efficient and low-stress environment.

Ensure those above you are finding success

I've spent so much time here fighting against sycophancy (being a suck-up, a yes-man, etc.), that this piece of advice may

The Critical Step of Choosing a Boss

It seems like a fallacy to say that you choose your boss, and that is often the case. Management changes and you don't control who your manager is when there is an organizational change.

However, when you are looking for new work, or thinking about moving into middle management, it behooves you to do some research on your potential manager. For a new job, make sure that your potential boss is one of the interviewers, and if not—ask for that. It's not a good sign when the person who will be your boss isn't doing the interview.

When you are looking to move into middle management, ask around the company and find the best respected middlers and use your networking skills to get into that shop if you can.

Even if you can't choose your boss, you can walk into the relationship with eyes wide open. Does she exhibit the seven behaviors of great middlers? How does she do at the six calibrations? What is her credibility on the street?

seem to undermine my message. But the fact is, you need the endeavor to succeed, but you also need the individuals above you to succeed. Now, if you have great internal alignment to the Greater Good, this should be easy. But on the surface, this can be extremely self-serving: their promotion opens opportunities for you. But it also creates an environment of trust if you are dedicated to the success of those above you. Just as importantly, your team sees that and notes the behavior.

Network horizontally

A strong middle worker spends a considerable amount of time working on and strengthening the connective tissue of a company. That means connecting up and down. But one of the great ways to ensure that large endeavors get the right results is to take the time and invest the energy to network horizontally, not just vertically.

This means looking across at the same performance level and find others in your relative position across all the different divisions and engage in team building activities and networking. Find out what they are working on and see if you and your team can help. Invest in these relationships.

It takes effort and you have a lot of things you are doing. But this pays dividends and creates relationships that will serve you well in the future.

Respect the position you are in

One last note on the better Middle, and an important one as we talk about the act of moving further up in an organization and preparing yourself for greater responsibility, leadership and directing. What I want to conclude with is this: respect the position you are in.

If you consider the work you are currently doing merely a stepping stone to another more fulfilling, higher-paying, or more challenging position, I can guarantee you one thing: it shows. Your team will sense it. So will your boss.

I spoke earlier of stating your intentions and acting the part before you have it. But first and foremost, you must respect the work you are doing and do it well. This dedication and respect will show through and get you where you are going faster than acting like a short-timer looking for a move as soon as possible.

Conclusion

Moving through the Middle

I'm almost done. I promise. The important part of this book is behind you now: the seven behaviors of great middlers and the six calibrations. You are comfortable identifying great middlers, and even have great steps to follow to make the move into the middle.

Great. But now it's time to consider that final frontier: what if I'm ready to move past the middle?

Moving through the Middle

Leaving the ranks of the middle and becoming a leader at the tops of organizations is a powerful, humbling and challenging task. I won't spend too much time on this subject, as it is covered in great and lasting detail in leadership books that line the shelves both real and virtual. What I don't think is well covered is asking the question, do you really want to be at the top? I know that I've had to ask myself that question many times and it is not a straightforward answer.

First, I think many people believe that getting to the top of the corporate ladder is precisely what global corporate careers are all about. If you are not trying to get to the top, then why are you even in the game?

Second, the questioning process typically revolves around work-life balance. Can I take on more accountability and still keep my life balanced? How will this impact my personal life?

Finally, the question becomes one of compensation and wealth. Will I be making more money? Is this a great package in terms of how much money I make?

These are all very real questions to ask about moving to the top. But I would challenge you to ask one more question:

Can I do more good for the company where I am now?

This, I'm sure, will always be a controversial question. Of course I can do more good if I have more power, more accountability and more leverage. But the truth is, sometimes a good leader is less influential than a great middle manager. And the skills are often not the same—it's not that different from moving out of the doer ranks and into the middler ranks. What makes you great in the middle isn't always what makes you great at the top.

Know the middle before you know top

In the context of this book, when you make the decision to move past the middle, the advice I give is this: no great leader can move sustainably to the top of an organization without a deep understanding of and respect for the middle of that organization. So the work you put in throughout the journey on this book remains important. Having the context of what a great middle looks like, and (even better) having the experience of being there and mastering the calibrations, will help you be a great leader and understand how to keep your sophisticated endeavors on track for success.

Because here's the final secret, which you probably aren't surprised by: you are always in the middle. Even a CEO is between this employees and the board. That CEO is calibrating activities between a customer base and a supply chain.

The work of successful endeavors is made of middles. Master the middle and you master the act of getting great results from teams.

Middlework: Breaking through the stereotypes

So that's it. I'm done for now. As a middle child and middle manager, it has been my intent to champion middlework as something more than the object of scorn and ridicule. Instead, the evidence suggests, and experience confirms, that no sophisticated endeavor succeeds without middlework. And middlework requires great people, armed with the seven behaviors, focused on the six calibrations.

No matter your current position in a company or endeavor, take a look around. Look at what needs to be done. Then unlock the secret of success by focusing on the middlework.

Bibliography

Armour, Stephanie. "Who Wants to be a Middle Manager?" USA Today. August 13, 2007. http://usatoday30.usatoday.com/money/workplace/2007-08-12-no-manage_N.htm

"Saving David Brent." The Economist, Schumpeter Column. April 15, 2011. http://www.economist.com/blogs/schumpeter/2011/08/middle-managers

Grafton, Lynda. "The End of the Middle Manager." Harvard Business Review, January 2011. http://hbr.org/2011/01/column-the-end-of-the-middle-manager/ar/1

Mollick, Ethan. "People and Process, Suits and Innovators: Individuals and Firm Performance." www.knowledge.wharton.upenn.edu. Wharton School of Management. March 2011.

Patterson, Kelly et. al. Crucial Conversations: Tools for Talking When Stakes Are High. Second Edition. McGraw-Hill, 2011.

Salmon, Catherine, PH.D, and Katrin Schumann. The Secret Power of Middle Children. New York, Hudson Street Press, 2011.

Tabrizi, Benham. "New Research: What Sets Effective Middle Managers Apart." Harvard Business Review, May 8, 2013. http://blogs.hbr.org/cs/2013/05/reinventing_middle_management.html?utm_campaign=Socialflow&utm_source=Socialflow&utm_medium=Tweet

Williams, David K. "The End of Middle Managers (And Why They'll Never Be Missed). " Forbes, July 10, 2012. http://www.forbes.com/sites/davidkwilliams/2012/07/10/the-end-of-middle-managers-and-why-theyll-never-be-missed/

Index

A

Act Decisively 7, 13, 46, 56. *See also* Seven Behaviors of Great Middle Managers
Area Vice President 15
Arise Virtual Solutions 20

B

Behavior Intensity 49
Bottom-up direction 14. *See also* Six Calibrations of Great Middle Managers
Brent. David 2
Budget 14, 29, 53, 63. *See also* Six Calibrations of Great Middle Managers
Budget changes 14. *See also* Six Calibrations of Great Middle Managers

C

calibration 7, 10, 13, 14, 19, 33, 46, 51, 53, 56, 61, 64, 72, 74, 77, 81, 92, 107, 110, 113. *See also* Six Calibrations of Great Middle Managers
CEO 17, 68, 115. *See also* Eye of Sauron
Choosing a Boss 110
C level 15, 68
Commit to Listening 7, 13, 31, 56, 85. *See also* Seven Behaviors of Great Middle Managers
corporate ladder 72, 73, 95, 96, 113
Corporate Title Grade Inflation 82
courage 7, 31, 44, 57, 80, 101, 109. *See also* Seven Behaviors of Great Middle Managers
Crack in the Door Dilemma 98
crackpot. *See* lean-agile crackpot
Craigslist 19
credibility 31, 42, 108, 110. *See also* street cred
CRM 38
cross-functional governance committee 57
crossroads 66
Crucial Conversations 31
current state 85, 86

D

da Vinci, Leonardo 11
dashboard 53. *See also* Six Calibrations of Great Middle Managers
diagnostician 30, 119
DiFranco, Ani 41
Diplomacy 37, 40
Diplomacy as firefighter 40
Diplomacy as fire retardant 37
Director 15, 42, 49, 50, 72, 82, 92, 109
Display Courage 5, 7, 13, 44, 56, 73. *See also* Seven Behaviors of Great Middle Managers, Courage
Diversity 23
Durden, Tyler 1

E

Ebay 19
Eisenhower, Dwight D. 104
emotional IQ 31, 57
emotional state 32
endeavor 4, 6, 7, 9, 12, 20, 23, 29, 40, 53, 67, 68, 80, 96, 100, 111, 114, 115
entitlement 6, 96, 99, 100
Eye of Sauron 17. *See also* CEO

F

Facebook 105
fact-driven 30, 49. *See also* Seek Reality
fact-gatherer 29. *See also* Seek Reality
fact synthesizer 30. *See also* Seek Reality
field manager 16, 69. *See also* line manager
Fight Club 1
final frontier 113
Finger-wag trap 54
flexibility 3, 7, 45, 50, 56, 92. *See also* Seven Behaviors of Great Middle Managers
Focus on the Greater Good 5, 13, 24, 50, 56, 76. *See also* Greater Good, Seven Behaviors of Great Middle Managers

four dimensions 6, 83. *See also* Organizational Structure

G

glue 4, 9, 20, 68
Google 19
Greater Good 5, 7, 13, 24, 45, 49, 56, 65, 71, 81, 101, 110. *See also* Focus on the Greater Good, Seven Behaviors of Great Middle Managers

H

Herbert, Frank 44
HIPPO 61
humility 45, 96, 99. *See also* Remain Flexible

I

IC. *See* Individual Contributors
Individual Contributor Career Path 99
Individual Contributors 2, 6, 10, 15, 79
intended message 32
internalize that Greater Good 28. *See also* Greater Good
Inter-team cohesion 14, 59. *See also* Six Calibrations of Great Middle Managers
Intra-team cohesion 14. *See also* Six Calibrations of Great Middle Managers
introvert 102
Ive, Jony 3

J

judgment 45–50. *See also* Act Decisively

K

Kaizen 84
Kings of the Middle 6, 75, 77. *See also* Vice President

L

leadership 2, 6, 17, 26, 54, 76, 111, 113
Lean 62, 84
lean-agile crackpot 60
line manager 16, 50, 68, 78, 90
LinkedIn 105
listener 31, 34, 36
long-term goals 95

M

Maintain Composure 7, 13, 36, 56, 73. *See also* Seven Behaviors of Great Middle Managers
matrix management 10, 88, 89
micro-management dysfunction 19
middleborn 3
middle child 1, 3, 115
Middle Child Syndrome 2
middleman 20
middle management 1, 4, 7, 11, 15, 17, 23, 64, 67, 71, 73, 99, 107, 110
middle manager 2, 11, 19, 23, 25, 28, 30, 36, 43, 46, 59, 61, 64, 68, 96, 99, 109, 114. *See also* middle management
middler 7, 9, 11, 13, 17, 27, 30, 37, 42, 51, 53, 57, 59, 65, 68, 95, 106, 113
Middlework 9, 14, 19, 37, 67, 76, 79, 81, 115
mind-killer 44
Mollick, Ethan 2, 4
Moneyball-ization 61
Monster.com 2

N

negative space 34
Networking 7, 102, 106. *See also* Visibility

O

organizational level 4. *See also* organizational structure
Organizational Structure 6, 83, 88

P

Patterson, Kerry et. al. 31
people managers 88, 90. *See also* matrix management
performance reviews 17, 18, 78
planning 60, 104
plateaus 86. *See also* Four Dimensions
positive intent 36, 40
Product Manager 16, 81, 83, 89
Program Manager 80, 97
Project Management Office 79
Project Manager 16, 78, 85
pushover 45

R

Remain Flexible 7, 13, 45, 56, 73. *See also* Seven Behaviors of Great Middle Managers, Flexibility

S

Salmon, Catherine, PH.D 1, 3
Schumann, Katrin 1, 3
scrum master 34
The Secret Power of Middle Children 1
Secretary Trap 79
Seek Reality 7, 13, 28, 56, 76. *See also* Seven Behaviors of Great Middle Managers
selflessness 25
Senior Director 15, 49, 50, 82
Senior Manager 16, 68, 71, 73, 78, 92
Seven Behaviors of Great Middlers 13
short-timer 112
Simplicity 11
Six Calibrations of Great Middle Managers 7, 14, 30, 65, 92, 107, 110, 113, 115. *See also* Calibration
Six Sigma 84
span of control 83, 89, 92
stakeholders 48, 62
steady state 85
street cred 42, 108
suck-up 37, 110. *See* sycophancy
sustaining relationships 105
SWAT 26, 27
sycophancy 37, 45, 109

T

telecommunications 26
Timeline 14, 53, 64. *See also* Six Calibrations of Great Middle Managers
Timelines and Deadlines 14, 53, 64. *See also* Six Calibrations of Great Middle Managers
Top-down direction 14. *See also* Six Calibrations of Great Middle Managers
Twitter 105

V

video game industry 2
Visibility 102, 105. *See also* Networking

W

Williams, David K. 2
work managers 88, 90. *See also* matrix management

X

XY Theory of Management 12

Y

yes man 37, 110. *See* Sycophancy

Other Titles by Matthew Hart

The Last Iteration of Dexter Maxwell

The Last Iteration Of Dexter Maxwell is the first book in a series that takes the reader on an exciting journey to find out who Dexter Maxwell really is. The novel explores the intersection of different technologies and how they evolve subject to one another, and the intersection of science and faith. There are implicit thematic elements of sustainability and balance, and on the influence of information technology. -- Dex knows first-hand how tough it is living on the edge of a thoroughly technologized civilization in Grenver, Colorado. But it also has its perks. With his small league of street-smart outcasts, he's snarled the system with some of the most brazen stunts of the 22nd century. Not bad for an orphaned sewer rat that can't remember his childhood and will most likely end up iced for ages like any other criminal. No past, no future: no problem. As long as Dex has his friends and his mischief, he'll be alright. But after a botched stunt, Dex wakes up a foreigner in a brutal, bizarre underground city controlled by more than one shameless force-blind, a sword strapped to his back, and an old man telling him he's the vital component of the coming revolution. Dex can barely take in the reality of a new time before he's on the run, hunted by vicious assassins, and mixed up in a deadly plot a millennium in the making-and with the fate of two worlds at stake. -- Start an action-packed journey with THE LAST ITERATION OF DEXTER MAXWELL to find out who Dexter Maxwell really is. ADVENTUROUS SCIENCE FICTION SEASONED WITH SUSTAINABILITY.

Matthew Hart | Capscovil | December 14, 2012 | ISBN-10: 3942358301 | ISBN-13: 978-3942358309 | Edition 1

Oracle Enterprise Manager 10g

Protect your databases from hardware, software, and operator failures using the detailed information in this Oracle Press guide. Oracle RMAN 11g Backup and Recovery explains how to configure databases, generate accurate archives, and carry out system restores. Work from the command line or Oracle Enterprise Manager, automate the backup process, perform Oracle Flashback recoveries, and integrate cloud computing technology. This authoritative resource also shows you how to create reports, optimize performance, and implement third-party administration utilities.

Robert Freeman, Matthew Hart | McGraw-Hill Osborne Media | Oracle Press series | April 22, 2010 | ISBN-10: 0071628606 | ISBN-13: 978-0071628600 | Edition 1

Oracle RMAN 11g: Backup and Recovery

Master Oracle Enterprise Manager 10 g Grid Control Centralize and simplify enterprise infrastructure administration using the detailed information contained in this Oracle Press guide. Oracle Enterprise Manager 10g Control Handbook shows you how to implement a grid-based management system and maintain on-demand access to critical services. Develop rollout plans, configure hardware and software, deploy targets and agents, control access, and distribute business reports. This authoritative resource also explains how to generate reliable backups, implement top-down performance monitoring, and maximize system availability.

Werner De Gruyter, Matthew Hart, Daniel Nguyen | McGraw-Hill | Oracle Press series | March 22, 2010 | Edition 1

About the Author

Over the course of three decades in the workforce, Matthew Hart has been a vice president, director of software engineering, development manager, database diagnostician, librarian's assistant, bookstore clerk, paperboy, and at all times, a writer. He founded Matthew Hart Consulting in 2012 to help companies and individuals transform for better results.

Middlework is Matthew Hart's first management book. He has been writing technology books for McGraw-Hill since 2001. Capscovil Books published his first work of fiction, ***The Last Iteration of Dexter Maxwell***, in 2012. Book 2 of the Last Iteration series is due in November 2013.

Matthew lives in Kansas City, MO. You can find him on Twitter, Facebook, and the web at Matthew-Hart.com.

Made in the USA
Charleston, SC
07 June 2013